Student Handbook

Business Communication *for* Secretarial Certificates

Jon Sutherland
Diane Canwell

Heinemann Educational Publishers,
Halley Court, Jordan Hill, Oxford OX2 8EJ
a division of Reed Educational & Professional Publishing Ltd

Heinemann is a registered trademark of Reed Educational &
Professional Publishing Limited

OXFORD FLORENCE PRAGUE MADRID ATHENS
MELBOURNE AUCKLAND KUALA LUMPUR SINGAPORE TOKYO
IBADAN NAIROBI KAMPALA JOHANNESBURG GABORONE
PORTSMOUTH NH (USA) CHICAGO MEXICO CITY SAO PAULO

First published 1997
2000 99 98 11 10 9 8 7 6 5 4 3 2 1

A catalogue record for this book is available from the British Library
on request.

ISBN 0 435 45556 7

Designed by Jackie Hill
Typeset and illustrated by TechType, Abingdon, Oxon
Printed and bound in Great Britain by The Bath Press

Dedication

Dedicated to John and Emma

Contents

Introduction

The aim of this book is to investigate and explain the principles and processes involved in communications within an organisation. In addition to this we also look at the typical communications methods used and provide opportunities for the learner to practice these different forms of communication. It is hoped that we have illustrated the fact that an efficient and effective organisation needs to have effective communication systems in place, but also must continually review them in order to ensure that communication flows occur both up and down the organisation as well as between individuals who work together.

Each chapter in Business Communication provides an overview of the different functions in a business organisation and the types of communication used, supported by a variety of oral and written activities.

The final section of the book provides you with the opportunity to work on mock written examination papers and oral assignments in the same format as those you will meet in the exam.

Business Communication has been specially written for students studying for *Business Communication Stage II*, a core module of the RSA Certificate in Administrative and Secretarial Procedures, and *Use of English*, part of LCCIEB's Secretarial Studies Certificate. The book also reflects the requirements of GNVQ key skills in Communication at Level 2 for business students.

The book provides a vital source of information for those who are in work or preparing to work in a role which demands a competent level of communication. It is also hoped that the book will provide the reader with a useful guide to be able to improve their own communication skills and contribute more effectively to the operations of an organisation.

Whether you are using this book in your studies towards a secretarial certificate or as a practical guide to aid you in your job role, we hope that you find the information valuable.

We wish you luck in your studies or personal development.

Jon Sutherland
August 1997

Business organisations and structures

■ Introduction

The structure of an organisation will determine the channels through which communication is made. Information needs to flow freely around the organisation. In a small business it is easy for everyone to know exactly what is going on but, in larger organisations, the flow of information may be awkward and disrupted at various points.

In order to determine how effective the channels of communication are within an organisation, we must look at whether the right information has reached the right person at the right time. If there are any barriers that prevent this from happening, then they must be overcome in order to increase the effectiveness of that individual. The way in which an organisation is structured will often determine how hard or easy it is to get the information through to the right person. Organisations may need to consider fundamental changes in their structure if these barriers appear to be insurmountable.

Once the information has reached the correct person, it must be in such a format as to allow that individual immediate understanding. If the information is unclear, misleading or ambiguous in any way, then the channels of communication, however good they are, have been wasted.

Many basic forms of communication are applicable to both internal and external situations. The skills of communication are similar whether dealing with colleagues or customers. However, the different needs of these two groups may determine the exact style of the communication. Internal communications can very often be dealt with in an informal manner.

Communication channels

Open communication channels tend to be the sort where everyone within the organisation is at liberty to see and be aware of the information involved. Examples of open communication channels are:

- notice-boards
- newsletters
- minutes of meetings which are circulated to all staff
- non-confidential internal mail which is distributed openly
- multi-user systems, which offer significant advantages to an organisation in the case of non-restricted information. Access to this information via a multi-user computer system will involve the availability of numerous terminals throughout the organisation.

In order to ensure that all employees are aware of the limitations of access to restricted information, confidential labels or sealed internal post envelopes will be used. Obviously, if the organisation uses electronic mail systems for the communication of internal and external correspondence, then systems will be in place to ensure that monitors are not left switched on or displaying information whilst the employee is out of the office.

The communication systems of an organisation are particularly vulnerable in terms of security to unauthorised users. Communication systems rely on shared channels to transfer the information from machine to machine. The use of security codes has gone some way to address this problem. Other confidentiality and security devices in common use are those which allow limited levels of access into the system. By means of a security code numbering system, individuals can only gain access to limited numbers of levels of the system.

■ Methods of communication

The most effective method of communication will be chosen for transmitting messages in an organisation. This may take the form of the spoken word, which can include non-verbal communication, or the written word. Figure 1.1 lists the alternative forms of written and spoken communications used in the workplace. The most appropriate method of communication depends on factors such as speed, cost, need for instant feedback or need for a written record. For instance, oral communication may be chosen over written communication if the message to be delivered involves a certain amount of tact which can be easier to transmit in a private interview than in a written letter.

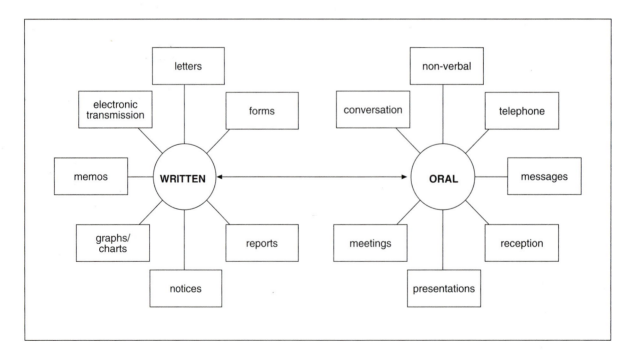

Figure 1.1 Communication methods

Models of communication

Any form of communication involves an exchange between a sender and a receiver. Obviously, these roles change and shift according to the nature of the communication process and the number of individuals involved. The characteristics of the sender and the receiver will have a marked impact on the communication process. The sender, for example, may have certain goals in mind when communicating with the receiver. The meaning and the balance of the message may be changed before it is passed on to another individual. On the other hand, the receiver may seek to misinterpret the message deliberately or place a different emphasis upon it. Both of these sets of circumstances could mean that the communication is distorted in some way and it is only when there are no vested interests that truly accurate communication can take place.

In most models of communication there will be references to transmitters and receptors, i.e. the means available for sending and receiving the messages. In effect, these are the media available to the individuals involved in the communication. Given the fact that all communications are restricted to a combination of the senses (see, hear, touch, smell and taste) there is only a limited variety of possibilities.

Messages

Messages include the data that is transmitted and the coded symbols that are an integral part of the message, designed to give particular meaning to the message. The sender will hope that any message sent will be understood by the receiver in as close a possible way to the original (or intended) meaning. The channels, as we shall see, are simply the means by which the messages are transmitted. These would include common business methods such as the telephone, the memorandum and the report. The other key aspect is 'noise'. This refers to the probable interference that may inhibit the message getting to the receiver in a clear manner. The normal response to this would be to try to cut out as much of the noise as possible or to communicate in such a way as to make the noise less intrusive, or simply to repeat the message until it has got through. This noise can refer to any number of circumstances or sets of conditions that can interfere with the message (including physical 'noise').

The sender attempts to transmit the message through a selected channel to the receiver's receptors. As we have already noted, these are the senses – the only way that the receiver can accept and respond to the message. The sender will need to encode the message in such a way that it can be readily understood by the receiver, or perhaps, in a specialised manner so that only a selected number of receivers can understand the message. This may be particularly useful if the sender only intends that a specific number or type of individuals understand the message.

Once an individual has received the message, it may need to be decoded. Through a shared language individuals are able to decode messages more accurately, leaving less chance for misunderstandings.

As we will see, most communication between a sender and a receiver is only the first stage of the process. The receiver may then become the sender, giving feedback in response to the original message. Feedback is a useful double-check for the original sender to make sure that the message was fully understood and the receiver's response is in line with what was expected as a probable response. The communication system should always be considered as a two-way process.

Student Activity

We will be considering the various methods of communication in detail throughout the book. Write down now as many different ways of communicating that you can think of. Figure 1.1 should help you.

Feedback/confirmation

With oral communication in, say, the giving of instructions or the provision of information, some kind of feedback is necessary to ensure that the recipient has understood what is being said or asked. This feedback can sometimes be just a 'yes' or a nod of the head but for the speaker this feedback is important. Alternatively, it can mean a telephone call to confirm receipt of a message or goods.

Feedback from any form of communication helps to cement the understanding of the recipient and to allow the sender of the message to feel secure that the correct information has been provided and that it will be dealt with.

In written communication, this can involve a letter sent to an organisation to confirm an order or the receipt of goods. It can also mean a letter to a hotel to confirm the accommodation arrangements made over the telephone, or to a travel agent confirming flight bookings made over a telephone.

■ Information technology and communication

Many organisations have recognised the need to use information technology effectively and to develop employee skills to handle its functions.

The skills required fall into two main categories – general and specialist skills.

- general skills – nearly all jobs have been affected in some way by the adoption of electronic technology. As a result, most employees must know in general terms how this technology works. Increasingly, technological systems have been integrated via a networking system and are no longer the relatively simpler stand-alone desktop PC
- specialist skills – nearly one per cent of the working population can now be considered to have specialist technology skills in relation to the use of

computers. Specialists will have particular skills in one or more computer functions, and may include the following:
– word processing
– desktop publishing
– data base
– spreadsheet
– graphics.

Benefits of IT

Technology has transformed businesses and many benefits have resulted. These benefits include the following:

- cost reductions
- simplified and efficient work flows
- increased responsiveness to customer needs
- additional job satisfaction
- opportunity for employees to learn new skills.

Tasks

Computer systems enable an individual to carry out the following main tasks, which include:

- recording information
- checking information
- sorting and classifying information
- summarising data
- calculating financial data
- storing and retrieving information
- reproducing information
- communicating information to remote terminals.

Specifically, these processes are covered by the following functions:

- **word processing** – the main function of a word-processing package is the manipulation, storage and retrieval of text. In addition, a modern word-processing system will allow graphics to be inserted into the text and via a database will provide names and addresses for mail-shots
- **desktop publishing** – DTP systems have been developed by merging the functions of word-processing and graphics packages. On a DTP system the operator has the facility to use a variety of different typefaces, fonts and styles in conjunction with various illustrations. It is possible to produce a very professional document using a DTP package
- **data base** – the storage of information is important to most business organisations. The construction of a data base that will provide the information you require needs careful consideration. When constructing a data base the designer must know what information will be required from the data base and what information needs to be input into the data base in order to fulfil these demands. The data base is capable of producing

Student Activity – Use of English

It is important that you get into the habit of checking or proof-reading typed text for accuracy. The following text contains 12 errors. Can you find them all?

Once upon a time, chopping was a labor. Sleeves were rolled up, ther was huffing and puffing, as the cook set to weilding a cleever to reduce the size of a large joint of meat. She would pound sugar or spices to a powder with a pestle and morter, and rub fruits through a clothe to make a puree.

It is little wonder that labour-saving devises were greeted so enthusisticlly. Some were wierd, some practicle, but they mostly helped to lighten the load of the cooks who used them.

Now we have electric servents, with blades to chop, grind and great, and I, for one, appreciate them, but we must be careful that this doesn't make for boring meals.

Work roles

2

■ Organisational structure and management

There are many different types of organisational structure leading to great differences in communication methods and processes. Here we will look at hierarchical and matrix structures which dictate how decisions are made and how communication is organised throughout the business.

Different organisations have different levels or layers of staff. One with many levels has a hierarchical structure (sometimes called a pyramid structure). The best way to understand what a hierarchical structure looks like is to imagine a pyramid (see Figure 2.1). At the top of the pyramid are the owners or major decision-makers of the organisation. As we look further down the pyramid the shape of the organisation broadens as more employees are involved at each level.

An organisation with only two or three levels of staff is known as a flat structure. A flat organisational structure is a version of the pyramid-style structure, but with fewer layers. Such organisations are usually quite small and all the staff will know each other.

Another type of organisational structure, which is becoming more popular in certain industries, is the matrix structure (see Figure 2.2). This system allows for teams to be created that consist of a number of individuals from various different parts of the organisation brought together to undertake a particular

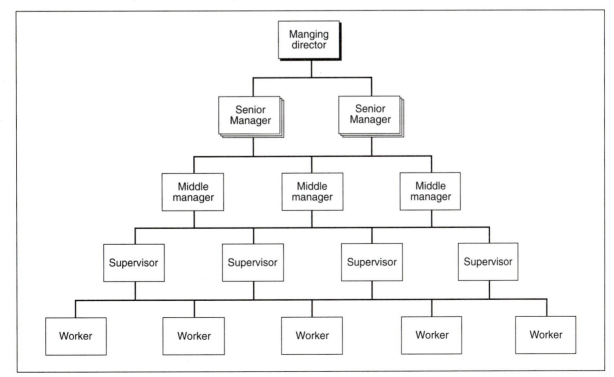

Figure 2.1 Hierarchial (pyramid) structure of an organisation

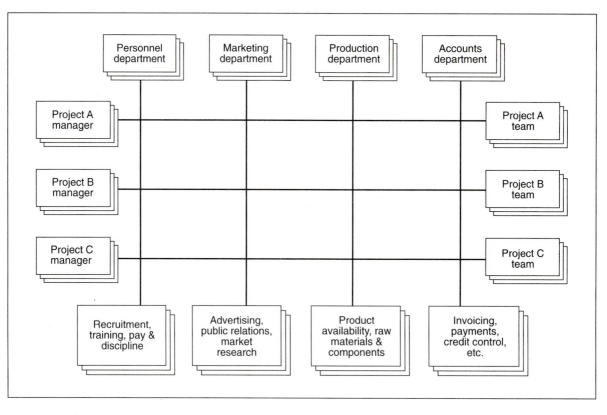

Figure 2.2 Matrix structure of an organisation

task. This can mean that individuals may have their regular manager to answer to, as well as the project leader. This system has the advantage of the team members being able to meet without direct reference to their departments. It also allows more individuals to be brought in to use their expertise when needed.

Lines of communication

A pyramid-style organisational structure breaks down all activities into specialised tasks and the decision making is made by the senior managers. All employees have very definite job roles and descriptions and communication is carried out on a vertical basis, from superior to subordinate. It takes the form of instructions based on decisions made by the senior management.

A matrix-style structure stresses the importance of teamwork, open communications and tends to allow decisions to be made at different levels of the organisation. Communication is both vertical and horizontal according to need. It can take the form of information requests and advice between the various levels of the organisation.

Communication channels

Communication channels run up and down the organisation, but they also run across the organisation too. Broadly speaking, we can identify four different directions in which communication channels will run:

- the **downward channel** is used by managers to send messages to their subordinates. This is often a lean channel as it does not really encourage feedback from the receiver
- the **upward channel** is primarily used by subordinates to send their messages to the manager. This is really the only formal means of communicating with the manager (particularly the senior management). This type of channel is normally encouraged by the management as they see this as a way of staying in touch with the rest of the organisation. It gives the subordinates a chance to participate in the activities and the decision making of the organisation
- the **horizontal channels** are used when communication takes place between departments or individuals working at the same level of the organisation. These are either formal ways of communicating or are less formal (such as discussions). They are especially useful when the organisation wants to try to co-ordinate the activities of two or more departments of the organisation. This type of channel will help the managers solve common problems and share experiences
- the **informal channels** or **grapevines** are common in most organisations. The communication channel can be a complex one, with the information passing from one individual to another by social contact and interaction. Typically, employees say that they learn more about what is going on in the business at lunch time than they ever do from meetings, memos and newsletters. Another informal channel of communicating can be networking. It is currently more popular in the USA than in Britain, but is becoming more popular as people discover the benefits of networking contacts – particularly when looking for employment. Networking involves getting to know more people and communicating with them about areas of mutual concern.

Student Activity

The institution in which you are studying this course will have formal and informal communication systems, the same as any other organisation. In order to assess how effective these systems are, you should find out the following:

- Do you have a course tutor? How often do you see your tutor on a formal basis? What do you have to do if you have a grievance? Is there a formal grievance procedure you can follow?
- What does a member of the staff have to do if he or she has a complaint about a student?
- Do you receive regular newsletters or student literature?
- Do you have a student union or guild?

message, regardless of how busy the work situation is, he or she should take steps to provide feedback to the sender of the message. This feedback may simply be a reply to say that the message has been received and is being dealt with. Alternatively, when written communication is involved, this may take the form of a written acknowledgement to say that the letter, memorandum or letter of complaint is being dealt with.

■ How to be a better communicator

The five main types of communication skills are:

- listening
- speaking
- face-to-face communication
- reading and writing
- the use of information technology.

To be a good communicator takes practice and experience, but some tips can be learnt and applied by everyone.

Listening

During the course of a day, we may listen to a number of different people. It is a rare person who will remember everything that has been said. This is particularly the case if the way in which conversation is listened to is unstructured and confused. In order to listen as effectively as possible, the individual must:

- actually hear the message itself
- interpret the message
- evaluate the message
- act upon the message and make use of the information it contains.

It is often a good idea to take notes during a conversation. Some people find it very helpful to use a tape recorder.

Speaking

Speaking need not necessarily take place face to face. It may also take the form of a telephone conversation. The use of questioning techniques is important in clarifying the exact nature of the message. In order to be an effective communicator the individual should:

- clearly know his or her role in the conversation
- be aware of the receptiveness and interest of those listening
- in some cases, be aware of the listener's own knowledge of the subject of the conversation.

It is not just what you say but how you say it that is important. Enhance your communication skills by taking note of the following:

- try not to speak too quickly or too slowly

- use the right words for the situation and do not be too complicated or simplistic
- listen to what the other person is saying in order to respond properly
- show confidence – both in yourself and in what you say
- try to put the other person at ease
- think about what you say and try to make your responses logical and easy to follow
- try to use the right tone for the situation, do not be too aggressive or passive or allow your feelings to confuse what it is you have to say
- if you have a strong or broad regional accent, try to talk slightly more slowly than normal
- never interrupt someone who is speaking
- take care to use the right tone of voice, as this can affect how the other person receives what is said. The same statement may be either acceptable or unacceptable, depending on the tone.

Student Activity

In order to assess your level of skill in listening and speaking, you should carry out the following role play exercise.

In pairs, taking alternate turns to play each role, you should recount to your partner something that has happened to you in the recent past. This could be a day out, a holiday, a visit somewhere or a television programme you particularly enjoyed. Your talk should last approximately 3 to 5 minutes. Once you have finished talking, ask your partner to relay back to you the content of your talk. How right was your partner? Was your partner a good listener? Were you a good communicator? Now change roles.

Face-to-face communication

A conversation, talk or discussion either within an office environment or on a personal level, is also known as face-to-face communication. Although recent telecommunication and technological advances have improved the way organisations can converse with each other, there is no real substitute for effective face-to-face communication and it is the most important way that individuals can communicate with one another. An element of non-verbal communication is always involved. We look in some detail at the different ways we communicate non-verbally with one another in the next section.

There are a wide variety of situations within an office environment which involve face-to-face communication, including:

- private or sociable discussions which take place within a particular office or section of the business
- brief 'chats' which take place in corridors or during lunch breaks
- formal and informal meetings

- when entering into conversation with customers and clients in person over a reception desk or retail counter
- when giving or receiving instructions
- when beginning or closing an interview with a potential job applicant.

Student Activity

How many other situations can you think of which would give the opportunity for talks or discussions on a face-to-face basis?

Obviously, the context of the discussion will determine the kind of language used and the extent and length of the talk. Regardless of the context, people often prefer this method of communication because they can get instant feedback from the other people involved in the conversation. The term discussion sometimes gives the impression of a heated debate, but this is not always the case. A simple discussion could involve talking about the previous night's television programme or a football match.

Student Activity

Working in groups of six, make a list of possible discussion topics for your own group. Choose one from the list and discuss it for 15 minutes. Did you find this an easy process or did it feel as if you had been asked to enter into a debate? Write down how you felt during the conversation and then compare your feelings with those of the rest of your group.

Reading and writing

These two skills are dealt with together since the writer of the message must be sensitive to how the message will be received by the reader. To be an effective writer an individual must take the following facts into account when presenting information:

- it will be read by a variety of people in different situations
- complex information needs to have sufficient background description in order to make it clear
- it should be capable of having a long life, in the sense that the information may be referred to many times in the future.

As with many other forms of communication, the written word may suffer from being ambiguous. Even the most informal of messages needs to be clear. Organisations use standard formats for a variety of written communication. These systems have been designed to avoid ambiguity. Certain forms of written communication can be easier to understand than others, but the writer should ensure that the reader always has sufficient information in order to form an opinion if required. The presentation of data, for example, should be carefully considered since financial information, in particular, can often be misleading or unclear.

Information technology

Information technology has transformed the way in which much information is processed, handled and distributed. The availability of computer facilities throughout organisations has meant that information can be relayed quickly and effectively. This is, of course, vital to the success of a business, but does require that individuals within the organisation be sufficiently trained on many different computer software packages.

■ Simple letters (and letter layout)

Most business organisations spend a considerable amount of their time communicating with their customers. Some of this communication, as we have already seen, will take the form of face-to-face or verbal communication. However, it is essential that some of these communications are supported by written evidence of agreements made.

In all organisations, neat, accurate and reliable written communication is vitally important. Organisations are usually concerned about how others view them. The view of external organisations will be affected by the way in which they receive information from that organisation.

A business letter is a communication that will be sent outside the organisation. Letters may be sent to obtain information from potential customers, to contact

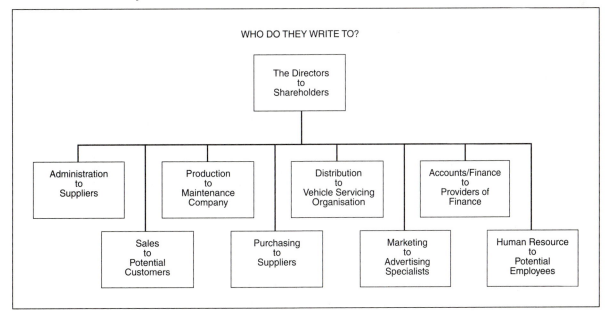

Figure 2.3 Letters need to be sent to a variety of people

the press in order to advertise products or services, to contact customers informing them of a new product or service and to contact potential employees who have completed job application forms. Figure 2.3 outlines some further individuals and/or organisations which departments may write to when providing information. It is important that such letters are neat, accurate and well presented. The headed paper used by the organisation for its business letters will form part of its corporate image. It will give the information an organisation would wish each of its customers or clients to see regularly. This includes the following details:

- name and address of the organisation
- telephone number and fax number of the organisation
- registered address of the organisation, as this may be different from the postal address
- company registration number
- names of the directors of the organisation
- any other companies the organisation may represent or be affiliated to.

Student Activity

Working on your own, and using Figure 2.3 as a starting point, think of as many other individuals or organisations as possible with which each department would communicate using the written word. Compare your list with those of the rest of your group.

The layout or format of the business letter will usually also be part of the organisation's corporate image, and different organisations have their own rules about the way in which a letter should be displayed. It is common to use the fully blocked method of display which means that each part of the letter starts at the left-hand margin. Open punctuation is also commonly used which means that the only parts of the letter to have punctuation are the paragraphs of text.

A business letter will be ordered in a certain way to contain all the necessary information. As well as the name and address of the organisation sending the letter, it needs to have the name and address of the recipient, the date and usually a reference, which can be the initials of the writer; sometimes there will also be a subject heading within the letter and if the letter is urgent, or confidential, this will appear at the beginning of the letter. If the recipient's name is known it is usual to address someone by their title and surname (not their initials). If the name of the recipient is not known the letter will start with 'Dear Sir or Madam' and end 'Yours faithfully'. If the person's name is known the letter will start 'Dear Ms Smith' (for example) and end with 'Yours sincerely'. The printed name of the person sending the letter (and their job title) will appear after the complimentary close, leaving enough room for the sender's signature. If the sender is unable to sign the letter, the secretary may sign it on behalf of the sender and include the letters 'pp' before the sender's printed name. If the letter includes any additional items, this is indicated at the end of the letter by the word 'Enc' or 'Encs' for more than one enclosure.

When a letter continues on to a second page, it is usual to use plain paper and provide details of the page number and date at the top of the second page.

Structure of a business letter

When writing a business letter, it is worthwhile remembering that it should have a beginning, middle and end. The beginning should briefly state the

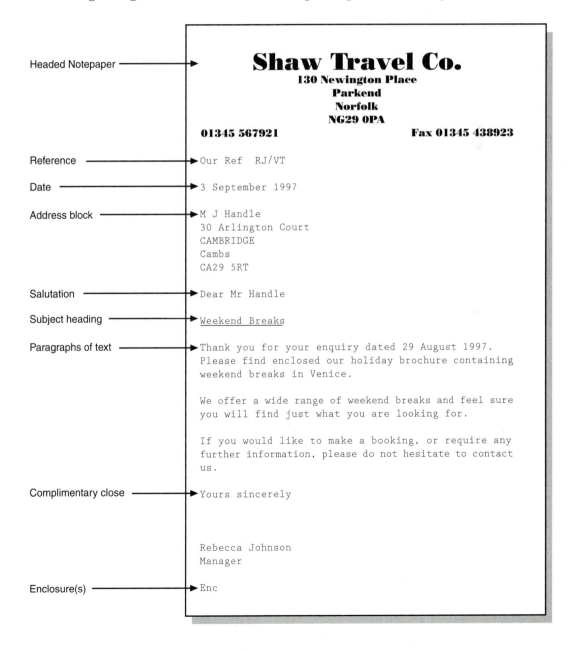

Figure 2.4 An example business letter

Student Activity

Imagine that you have been asked to write a letter of confirmation to a hotel for a booking which has been made over the telephone. Write a letter including the following details:

- use today's date
- the address is: Hotel Davenport, 25-30 Link Street, London W2B 9DF
- the booking has been made in the name of Mr Jones for the night of 24 April. He requires a single room with en-suite facilities on a bed and breakfast basis, for one night only.

Student Activity

You have been asked by your tutor to write to a local business person who is coming to your college to give a talk on career prospects in his industry. Your tutor has asked you to send a map of the college and to confirm the date and time of the visit, which is on 4 October at 3.00 pm. Write the letter to: Mr J.S. Lee, Technical Manager, Johnsons Plastics, Mill Road, Anytown AN1 5RU. Use you own name and college address and the heading 'Career Visit'.

reason for writing and may refer to a previous letter, contact or document. The middle provides the recipient with details of the information you wish to impart. It may involve giving instructions or asking for information. This may consist of one or more paragraphs and numbered bullets can be used to break down detailed information. The end of the letter can be used to review what has already been said, which may include any action the sender will take or action you wish the recipient to take. The final sentence is usually a simple, relevant closing statement. For example: 'I look forward to hearing from you soon.' 'If you require any further information, please let me know.' 'If you have any queries, please let me know.'

■ Memos (the simple memo and memo layout)

Internal memoranda are used for communication between different departments within the same organisation. They are often called memos. They are usually shorter than a business letter and deal with one particular subject. When more than one point is being made it is normal to number them. Memos are not signed in the same way as a business letter, but the person issuing the memo would normally initial it at the end.

Many organisations use pre-printed memorandum paper (see Figure 2.5) in much the same way as they use their letterhead paper. The exact style of the

MEMORANDUM

To   Mary John
From   Rose Taylor
Ref   MJ/RT
Date   15 May 1997

Figure 2.5 An example of pre-printed memorandum paper

memo will depend on the corporate image of the organisation, but all will need to be clearly marked and dated (often including a reference for filing purposes). For this reason, a memo format will always include the following headings: to, from, date, subject. The clear format means that information can be passed on quickly but in a more formal way than in a note.

However, as it is an internal method of communication a memo is usually written in a relatively informal style. The sender of the memo may know the recipient(s) and so a formal manner is not necessary or appropriate. However, the sender must be aware of who the recipient is and their hierarchical status in the company.

A memo can be compared with a business letter in the following ways:

- both should always be dated
- the reference will indicate where the document is to be filed and will serve as a future reference in further communication
- the words *confidential*, *private and confidential*, *personal* or *urgent* can be applied to both letters and memos
- enclosures and attachments will be indicated on both letters and memos
- although a memorandum does not include a signature, it is sometimes initialled by the sender
- continuation sheets are numbered on plain paper.

As with a business letter, a memo should be structured by providing background information (reason for writing) to begin with. Then the proposed action should be separated into paragraphs and the memo can be ended with a short review of what has been proposed or asked for.

Student Activity

Imagine that you are working in the sales department of an organisation. You have a new member of staff joining in one month's time and a new filing cabinet and a desk will be needed. Send a memo to the purchasing department of your organisation and ask them to order the above for you. You need the furniture to match that already being used in the department.

Student Activity

Your employer has asked you to write a memo to all staff in your section concerning the way A4 paper is being wasted. She is very concerned that too many hard copies of documents are being printed and then not used. Apparently the stationery bill has increased by 17.5% in the last three months and this is causing problems with the departmental budget.

■ Use of English

In our everyday lives, we need to use written communications, and it is just as important when writing a personal letter to a friend or a note to one of the family as in business correspondence that the spelling and grammar are correct.

The apostrophe

The apostrophe is commonly used in written communication and often causes confusion. Many people use it wrongly. It is used in two different ways:

- to show that a letter or letters have been **missed out** of a word, i.e. to shorten it
- to show that something **belongs** to someone or something, i.e. possession.

The first use of the apostrophe can be seen, for example, in *isn't* instead of *is not*: the apostrophe goes where the 'missing o' is. Another example would be *I'm* instead *I am*.

The second use of the apostrophe is to show ownership; for example, *The manager's car,* i.e. the apostrophe indicates that it is the car belonging to the manager. Remember that if, in this example, two managers shared one car the apostrophe would go after the 's', i.e. *The managers' car.*

There is one important exception to this possessive use of the apostrophe, which is with the word *it*. When you see *it's* it always means *it is* and the belonging use is always *its,* **without** the apostrophe. For example, 'It's a good car but its paintwork is in a poor condition.'

Student Activity

Try this task – place the apostrophe in the appropriate position in the following sentences:

- Jaynes desk
- The directors office
- The dog licked its paw
- The girls coats
- The girls couldnt find their pens and pencils
- Its a nice day today isnt it

Plurals

As with apostrophes, you will need to show words in plural in written communication. A plural of a word means 'more than one', so the plural of *dog* is *dogs*. A plural is usually formed simply by adding an 's', as in the example of 'dogs'. However, some words can be both singular (one) and plural, such as 'sheep'. Other words need more than just 's' to transform them into a plural. For example, words ending in '-y', such as 'library' or 'facility', require *-ies* in place of the '-y' ending, to make them plural; i.e. *libraries* and *facilities* and words ending in '-s' usually add '-es' at the end.

The following nouns drop the ending '-f' or '-fe' and add the ending '-ves' in the plural: calf, half, knife, leaf, life, loaf, self, sheaf, shelf, thief, wife, wolf.

Foreign words in our language require special attention and often need to be learnt individually.

Student Activity

Write the plurals of the following words:

donkey	record
family	jacket
ability	paper
gateau	embarass
architecture	knife

Check your answers in a dictionary.

Verbs

A verb is a word which describes an action. It is sometimes known therefore as a 'doing' word. For example; 'The manager *opened* the door'. A sentence is not complete without a verb. For example; 'The new office layout a big success'. This does not make complete sense without the missing verb – *is*. The doing or active words in a sentence are therefore usually the verbs.

Student Activity

How many of the following words are verbs?

travelling	running
monitoring	walking
enormous	photographic
highlight	telephone
generous	dancing
sensitive	lampshade
healthy	books

Indicate the ones you think are verbs. How do you know that they are?
If you are unsure check in the dictionary or discuss with your tutor.

Reception

3

■ Introduction

Here we will look at the rules and guidelines concerning the receiving and greeting of visitors to an organisation. This includes personal callers to the premises, as well as those clients or customers who may telephone to make an enquiry. We will cover here the main purpose and function of the reception facility, as well as the reasons why a visitor may be calling at the organisation.

■ Reception duties

There could be a great many reasons why visitors need to call – depending on the type and size of the organisation. We intend to look at personal callers in this section, dealing with telephone calls later.

Whatever the type of organisation, and regardless of its size, some visitors will call during the course of a normal working day. It is essential to the image and reputation of that organisation that all visitors are dealt with in an efficient, polite and courteous manner. Remember that seeing the reception area or receptionist is the first impression a prospective client or customer will have of that organisation. If the receptionist does not carry out an efficient job then sales can be lost.

Types of callers

It may be that the person calling at the premises of the organisation is a first-time caller, perhaps making an enquiry regarding the services or products of the organisation with a view to placing an order or negotiating a long-term contract. Because this is the first time this person has had contact with the organisation, it is very important that the impression given is a good one. The receptionist should deal with an initial enquiry in the following way:

- greet the caller promptly in a polite and courteous manner
- identify the best person to deal with the caller
- contact the person concerned to find out if they are free
- if the person concerned is free and willing to see the caller, the receptionist should direct the caller to the office in a clear and accurate manner
- if the person concerned is *not* free the receptionist should:
  - ask the caller if it is possible to wait, and, if so offer refreshment and magazines
  - ask the caller to make an appointment for another day/time
  - ask the caller if he or she would prefer to see someone else, and, if so, contact that person and direct the visitor to the appropriate office
- the receptionist should log the caller in the records and make a mental note of the name of the person so that another time the person can be greeted by name.

On a regular basis, the receptionist may have to deal with suppliers who are calling at the organisation. These suppliers may or may not be expected. Often sales representatives will make appointments to call at regular intervals to take orders for goods they sell. On the other hand, it may be that they will call simply because they are in the area. The receptionist will get to know different suppliers by name and know who they wish to see when they arrive. A good receptionist will also know whether the supplier is a welcome visitor to the organisation and should use tact and diplomacy if dealing with an unwelcome visitor.

Most suppliers will use a **business card** which will state their name and organisation plus their telephone and fax number. The receptionist should take the business card and contact the person the supplier has called to see. A supplier who has an appointment should be directed to the office concerned, or the receptionist should contact the member of staff the supplier wishes to see and make alternative arrangements.

Routine callers

Routine callers are usually those who are expected. The receptionist would be aware of the visit as it would have been logged in the **appointments book**. As the caller arrives for the appointment, the receptionist should carry out the following:

- greet the caller (by name if known) promptly, courteously and politely
- contact the member of staff the caller has an appointment with
- if the member of staff is available, direct the visitor clearly and accurately to his or her destination
- if the member of staff is not quite ready, ensure that the visitor is offered refreshment and is looked after while waiting
- deal immediately with all the documentation for the visit.

Student Activity

Using the appointments book in Figure 3.1, fill it in for the following, ensuring that they appear in the correct order using the 24-hour clock:

- Mr Thompson is expecting Mr Brundish to visit at 11.15 and then Mr Jennings at 3.00 in the afternoon. After Mr Jennings has left, Mr Thompson wants to see Mr Brundish again at 16.15.
- The Personnel Manager is expecting the following people:
  - Miss Dunne at 14.30
  - Ms Jackson at 10.15
  - Mrs Hollingsworth at 12.15
  - Susan Penhaligonn at 3.35
  - Brian Fortescue at 16.00

NAME OF CALLER	FIRM	TIME OF ARRIVAL	TO SEE	TIME OF DEPARTURE
Mrs. Johnson		10.30	Sales manager	

Figure 3.1 An example appointments book

Unexpected visitors

The receptionist should make every effort to ensure that a visitor who arrives without an appointment is seen by someone. The visitor should be offered several alternatives:

- are you prepared to wait to see the person you want to see?
- would someone else be able to help you?
- would you like to make an appointment for another day/time?

The receptionist's role is to bring the situation to a satisfactory conclusion for both the visitor and the organisation. Non-routine visitors are also logged by the receptionist in the visitors' book.

were to pass on the information *verbatim* (word for word) each time somebody left a message either by telephone or in a face-to-face situation. When taking a message for another individual, the following points should be remembered:

- listen very carefully to the message
- make notes as you listen
- your notes should contain key words and important information, such as the date and time of the call, and the name and details of the caller
- after you have taken the message, and before you pass it on to the recipient, write it out in a form that can be easily understood
- do not include any unnecessary information
- make sure you mention names, addresses, telephone numbers, fax numbers, order numbers and any deadlines to be met
- either telephone the message through to the recipient or pass on the relevant information face-to-face
- ensure that your tone and style is correct when both receiving and passing on the message.

Student Activity

Carry out the following role play in pairs, taking turns to be the bearer of the message and the recipient:

Message one – 'I'd like to speak to Miss Smith please. Oh isn't she, well can I leave a message then? Fine. Can you tell her that I was supposed to be coming in to see her next Friday, I think that's the 12th, yes it is. Well I'm afraid I shan't be able to make it then because I have a dental appointment at 11.00 and then I have to go down to London for a big sales conference we are holding there. Will you tell her that I can make the following week at 11.00 if that's OK with her. Perhaps she can ring me to confirm. My name's Claire Saunders and I'm with McIvortex on 01223 765765. Bye.'

Message two – 'Hello, can you put me through to Miss Smith please? Is she likely to be back today – my name is Somersgill? OK, well I'll leave a message then, but I really want to speak to her urgently. I am very disappointed with the delivery we had today. All the boxes had burst open and the goods are virtually destroyed. We ordered them three weeks ago on order number 12345 and they were £3,775.00. I need a replacement batch to be sent out today, otherwise our production will have to shut down. I'm very cross about this as it's the second time it has happened. Get her to ring me back as soon as she gets in will you? I'll be in the office until 3.00, after that she will have to speak to Brian Gillby, his extension is 271 and mine is 248. Our company number is 01256 776878.'

Meetings

4

■ Introduction

Meetings are held in all organisations. They can be informal or formal, requiring a range of communication methods and secretarial support. In this chapter we look at the different types of meetings and the production of written documentation required.

■ Different types of meetings

Formal meetings

Formal meetings are often governed by the *constitution* of the organisation. This means that when the rules of the organisation were written, they included those relating to the procedure for formal meetings. Organisers of formal meetings must ensure they have a sound knowledge of the procedures involved. Formal meetings include:

- **Annual General Meeting (AGM)**
As the name implies, these meetings are held once a year and are used to assess the trading or affairs of the organisation over the previous year. Officers, for example, the chairperson, secretary and minutes secretary are elected at the AGM for the coming year. AGMs are open to all shareholders of the organisation and 21 days' notice must be given prior to the meeting. If this notice is not given, it is not considered constitutionally correct to hold the meeting, therefore making it invalid.

- **Board meetings**
The directors of an organisation attend board meetings, which are chaired by the chairperson of the board of directors or that person's deputy. Any type of business can be discussed at these meetings, and they do not always have to be run in a formal manner – depending on the size and type of organisation, they can sometimes be regarded as informal.

- **Statutory meetings**
After a report has been circulated to all members, a statutory meeting is called so that the directors of the organisation and its shareholders can communicate. It is a requirement of the law that these meetings take place and, particularly in the case of local government committees, organisations are required by an Act of Parliament to hold them.

Informal meetings

As their name implies, informal meetings have no procedural rules. Informal meetings might be set up for a number of reasons, for example, so a group of people working on a particular project can get together to share progress to date. Secretaries are still usually asked to attend informal meetings, although they will not necessarily be documented in such a formal way. Perhaps some

3   Matters arising

There were no matters arising from the previous minutes.

4   Report from the Chief Safety Officer

Mr Mills reported that the recent Government legislation concerning Health and Safety at Work procedures would require some careful consideration.

The new procedures would be copied and distributed to all concerned. Mr Mills stated that he would like a sub-committee to be formed to study the legislation and report back at the next meeting.

Mr Taylor, Mr Brenner and Ms Oliver volunteered to form the sub-committee, and agree to meet on Tuesday 27 June 19..

5   Implications of possible new extension to the office block

Ms Oliver reported that she had seen the plans for the new office block and was concerned that not enough space had been allocated to each member of staff using that block.

After some discussion it was decided that Mr Mills would speak to the architects and report his findings to the next meeting.

6   Report on recent training sessions

It was generally felt that the training sessions were of value, and that they should continue. Mr Kane was attending his session at the present time, and once Ms Oliver had attended, then all staff had been involved. It was anticipated that these sessions would take place annually, and that all representatives should ensure they attend.

7   Any other business

Mr Parsons reported that there had been some problems with the installation of the new electronic typewriters. The location of some of the machines had meant that wires were trailing in a dangerous way. Mr Parsons had dealt with this problem and all now seemed to be working well and safely.

8   Date of next meeting

The date of the next meeting was set for Friday 27 July 19.. at 0930. The venue will be arranged.

Signed

Figure 4.3   An example of minutes of a meeting

form of numbered listing is used against each minuted item. The later distribution of the minutes helps those present by reminding them of decisions made and any actions which they personally have to take.

Certain organisations, in particular local authorities, must have their minutes available for public inspection. The details of any motions voted upon (see below) or amendments made to these motions must be clearly detailed in the minutes.

Minutes should be prepared in the third person and in the past tense. Verbatim minutes are neither necessary or required, but it is important that they are accurate and that the text contains 'reported' rather than 'direct' speech.

■ Use of English

Reported speech

We tend to use direct speech in informal everyday situations, for example:

'Jack said to me, "I didn't recognise you in that car".'

In reported speech the words are not repeated exactly as they are said but are reported.

For example: 'Jack said he did not recognise me in that car.'

Reported speech is used in formal situations, for instance when noting down in the minutes what is said at meetings. For example, in a meeting someone could say,

'I can get those figures for next week'.

This would be set down in the minutes as,

'X agreed to obtain the figures for next week'.

Reported speech also requires a change of tense, usually from the present to the past. For example:

Jack: 'I think that's a smart car' would be reported as:

'Jack said he thought it was a smart car.'

The verb *think* has been put into the past tense *thought*.

Their/there/they're

These three words sound the same but have different meanings. They are likely to occur when writing minutes of a meeting. It is easy to confuse them and use the wrong word, but this can make nonsense of a sentence. Remember:

- *Their* always means 'belonging to them'; for example, *their* work. It is the plural of *his, her, its*
- *They're* always means 'they are'; for example, *they're* going now
- *There* can be used to show a place or to indicate something ('there is...'); for example, *go over there.*

Student Activity – Use of English

Decide what is incorrect about the following sentences and rewrite them using the correct grammar:

The girl went their because she was the only one.

There happy to be doing that kind of work.

The new students said they have good qualifications.

The children has always enjoyed there time at the beach.

The boys' coat was very dirty when he returned back home.

Motions

A motion is a proposal at a meeting, in other words, an issue that needs to be discussed and then decided upon by those at the meeting. Motions that are voted upon are called *resolutions*. It is a good idea that all business should be introduced to the meeting in the form of either a motion or a resolution, as this will allow everyone to give their views about the issue in question.

Usually, motions will have to be written and signed by the proposer and supported by a seconder. If you have to propose or support a motion, you should prepare well for the meeting:

- make sure that you read all the minutes, reports, briefings and other documents relating to the committee or type of meeting
- make sure that you know all the people at the meeting, they may have a particular interest or objection to certain proposals or points of view. Remember that you may need the support of several people at the meeting to ensure that your motion is carried forward
- make sure that you plan for success, but prepare for failure. Try to put yourself into the minds of those that may oppose your motion. Come up with some criticisms of your proposal and work out how you would respond to them.

There will be occasions when you have to speak to a group of other employees and senior managers at meetings. Particularly when you are proposing a motion, and subsequently supporting it with further comment and opinion, it is worth taking the following points into consideration:

- listen before you follow up your initial comments, you will be able to assess the mood of the meeting and perhaps summarise your responses to a number of different criticisms
- if you want to be effective in a meeting, then choose the right time to make a contribution. See where the argument is going and then decide on the most appropriate point to say something. It is perfectly acceptable to say that you agree or disagree with comments that have already been made (this shows

that you have been listening). Equally, you may need to wait for the right moment when the meeting seems to be moving in your favour and then step in and say your piece

■ always be brief – if you spend a considerable amount of time explaining a point that the rest of the meeting understands, then you may lose their interest and sympathy for your case. Give examples where appropriate, but do not labour the point if the meeting seems to be following what you are saying

■ try to make constant references to what others have said. Not only will this give you the opportunity to incorporate views that did not occur to you at first, but it will also help you to gain allies at the meeting

■ the only way to get around reasonable and rational objections to your motion is to counter them with a strong argument that is convincing and well structured. Gentle persuasion is always more effective than resorting to unnecessarily critical comments

■ at times you may have no choice but to give in

■ always treat everyone politely and with courtesy, even if other people are not being very polite about what you are saying and never show outward signs of boredom, annoyance, loss of temper or clock-watching

■ always show the chairperson the greatest respect and remember never to interrupt, engage in private conversations or attempt to monopolise the meeting by being long-winded and overly complicated.

Student Activity

In groups of six, you are going to hold a meeting. You must elect a chairperson and a minutes secretary and prepare an agenda. You can choose the items on the agenda, but you could use this opportunity of holding a meeting to evaluate some aspect of the course you are studying. Each member of the group of six should have an input into the meeting. You should each contribute to the discussions which take place and each table a motion upon which you take a vote. At the end you should each write up your own copy of the minutes from the notes taken by the minutes secretary. How do the minutes differ?

■ The role of the secretary

Making arrangements for a meeting can be very time consuming. Even if the secretary deals with meeting preparations on a regular basis, it can mean a great deal of extra work.

Any arrangements which need to be made should be carried out well in advance of the meeting and are usually the responsibility of the secretary of the person calling or chairing the meeting. This secretary will be in close contact with the secretaries of all members attending the meeting.

It is the secretary who has to arrange meetings and to liaise with other secretaries regarding the dates and times convenient to all involved in the meeting. It is a good idea to have a checklist of 'things to do before the meeting' so that nothing is forgotten, and nobody is left out.

The checklist below gives an idea of the timing required and the items to be dealt with before a meeting, as well as those things that must be done on the day of the meeting and in the days following it. This would be necessary if your manager calls a regular meeting. The tasks would be done by the secretary of the person calling the meeting and who will be chairing it. Such a checklist would ensure the smooth running of the meeting from an administrative standpoint.

Meeting checklist

Two weeks before the meeting

- Check the date of the meeting (this is often arranged as the last item on the agenda of the previous meeting).
- Put the date in your diary and in the diary of your manager, so nothing else will get booked for that day and time.
- Liaise with the secretaries of those involved to arrange the time and venue of the meeting, plus any requirements for overnight accommodation.
- Book the meeting room – this may be a board room, a conference room or an office which is big enough to accommodate all those involved.
- Order any refreshments that may be required during the meeting.
- Discuss with your manager the items for the Agenda.
- Once the agenda has been agreed with the chairperson it can be typed ready for issue.
- Book the accommodation required.

One week before the meeting

- Notify the secretaries of those attending the meeting about the arrangements you have made. Send with this notification a copy of the agenda and any papers they may need to read before the meeting.
- Prepare the chairperson's agenda.
- Book any car parking requirements for those people travelling to the meeting.

The day before the meeting

- Collect together spare copies of the agenda.
- Get the minutes of the previous meeting from the file.
- Gather together any relevant papers and files concerning items on the agenda.
- Make a list of any people who have sent their apologies because they will not be able to attend the meeting.
- Make sure you have enough stationery for the meeting itself (writing paper, notebooks, and so on), plus an attendance sheet for people to sign.

The day of the meeting

- Confirm the parking arrangements
- Contact reception and notify staff of the names of the visitors expected.

- Arrange with the switchboard to re-route any calls whilst the meeting is in progress, unless they are emergency calls which can be taken in the meeting room.
- Make sure that the meeting room is ready before the allocated time for the meeting to start. Check for heating, lighting and ventilation. In addition, ensure enough seats are available.
- Arrange the writing paper/notebooks and pens/pencils at each seat around the table.
- If possible provide jugs of water and glasses around the table.
- Put a 'Meeting in Progress' notice on the meeting room door.
- Place the Apologies next to the chairperson's agenda, as this will be one of the first items on the agenda.
- Provide the chairperson with a copy of the minutes of the last meeting as these will be read at the start of the meeting.
- Ensure that all those attending the meeting sign the attendance sheet.
- Make sure to have available spare copies of the agenda and any other relevant paperwork.

During the meeting

The primary role of the secretary is to assist the chairperson. Usually the secretary sits on the right-hand side of the chairperson. Sometimes, if the minutes of the last meeting have not previously been circulated, the secretary will be called upon to read them.

The following are guidelines for a successful meeting:

- ensure that the chairperson signs the minutes of the previous meeting
- take the minutes of the meeting
- make sure that the company's safety and security procedures are complied with during the meeting
- answer the telephone if it rings
- help serve refreshments
- once the meeting has finished, clear the room and make sure all the paperwork is returned to the relevant files. Remember to remove the 'Meeting in Progress' notice from the door. The secretary should also:
  - notify switchboard that the meeting has finished
  - notify catering staff that the refreshment trolley can be collected
  - escort guests off the premises, if necessary.

The day after the meeting

- Prepare a draft copy of the minutes.
- Ask the chairperson to check and sanction the minutes and when they have been approved type them in their final form.
- Distribute the minutes of the meeting to those involved.
- Type any correspondence resulting from the meeting.
- File away any paperwork which was used for the meeting.
- Note in your diary the date of the next meeting.

5 Administration Department

■ Introduction

The administrative staff of an organisation are mainly concerned with providing an efficient and effective support service for other departments. Many of the documents that they deal with will be sent to them from staff in the following departments:

- sales
- marketing
- research and design
- purchasing
- accounts or finance
- personnel or human resources.

The communication process for the administration department must be efficient. It is essential that all the administrative systems provide an effective communication channel for the organisation as a whole.

■ Information processing in administration and secretarial duties

Depending on the type, size and nature of the organisation, the administration and secretarial staff may deal with a wide variety of different information from a vast range of sources. Information must be 'processed' into a form that is appropriate and useful. Typically, we can categorise the sources of information into two distinct areas:

- primary sources – this is information that has been generated by, or on behalf of, the organisation. It will include various financial data, such as sales figures, revenue and profit; operational information, such as stock levels, valuations, wastage and re-order levels; marketing information, such as responses from advertising, customer leads and marketing research data. Much of this information will be highly confidential and will require complete discretion from those who deal with it – mindful of the value that it might have to a competitor.
- secondary sources – these can include a variety of different sources, usually from outside the organisation. Typically, we can identify government statistics or data, information received from a marketing research company, or information about general trends and fashions, as examples of secondary data or information. This material will be less confidential, but the organisation may well have had to pay for it. The data often comes in a form that is not ideal for use and it may have to be compared with primary information in order to see its relevance and use.

■ Organising information from different sources

Just as you write a project for your course, so you may be asked by your employer to write a report. If this task is new to you, it may be useful to look at some guidelines.

- preparation – the first thing you need to find out is the date for completion of the report. Allow yourself plenty of time to research and write up the information.
- find out exactly what is required of you. How long does the report have to be? How many pages of typing or writing is expected? Is there a limit to the number of words submitted? Are you expected to offer conclusions drawn from the facts?
- do you have to submit the report in a certain format? Are there set headings you are expected to use?
- where will you find the information you need? Make a list of the sources of information you will need to use. Many organisations can offer assistance, it will obviously depend on the type of research you are carrying out.

Obtaining information from different sources

For the majority of tasks, the library will be the primary source of information. Your college or local library will give you access to vast amounts of knowledge and information, and each will employ staff who can help you. Many large organisations have their own library facility and specialists, but most other organisations would require their staff to use local libraries to find out specific information.

Libraries reference their material in a system called 'Dewey Decimal', which involves indexing the information by number under different topics or subjects. For example, all information relating to English is under number 600. Since technology has developed over the years, many libraries now catalogue their stock of books using a computerised system. Each library may use a different form of computerisation, but most store their supply of books either under the subject content or the name of the author.

Obviously, the type of information being researched will determine the primary source of information, but the following list indicates some of the more usual reference books used by administrative staff:

- dictionaries – for spelling and use of abbreviations. Some reference books also provide information regarding the correct use of English, for example *ABC of English Usage* and *Roget's Thesaurus*
- directories – such as the British Telecom telephone and fax directories. Other directories include the postcode and street directories
- guides and yearbooks – for example railway timetables and the different trade handbooks of specific professions, such as *The Medical Register*

- encyclopaedias and general reference books – including the *Encyclopaedia Britannica* and *Whitaker's Almanack*
- hotel and restaurant guides – including the *AA Guide to Hotels and Restaurants* and *The Good Food Guide.*

Student Activity

You are working with your manager on a report about sales of ice cream. Your manager has asked you to write to a local company which makes special ice creams for home consumption, to find out what last year's sales were. As you work for a retail organisation (i.e. not a competitor) you hope to get these figures but you must make it clear why you need the information.

Organising information

Before you can begin to write up your report you have to be sure that all the information you have collected is accurate, relevant, up-to-date and complete. Check all the details, especially dates, and discard any outdated information. You should cross-check your material for accuracy by referring to more than one source. Finally, organise your information by selecting all the relevant details you need in order to give a complete report *without* including any unnecessary details or irrelevant facts.

■ Synthesising information

When you have gathered and organised all the information necessary for your report, you will need to summarise it into a form suitable for presentation. There are a number of different ways of carrying this out, which are outlined below. It is important to remember that the summary of the information should be presented in such a way as to allow the reader to understand what is being said without the benefit of ever having seen the original information. A good summary means that you have reduced the 'bulk' of the information into a brief, but understandable format that can be quickly and easily read.

Summaries and précis

As part of your work you may be given the task of reading a long article or report and then presenting the information in a more brief and concise fashion. The original document could be long and complicated, so it is necessary to understand the information you read before you start. You would then take out the unnecessary details and write a summary of the information. The following guidelines will help with doing summaries.

- read through the whole document first, without trying to understand everything as you go through for the first time
- re-read the document more thoroughly. You could highlight the areas of importance at this stage, or cross out the unnecessary information

- make a list of the items you have to include and compare your list with the main document to make sure you have not forgotten anything important
- write a draft summary. It may be that a superior should check this for you at this stage. When you are happy with this attempt you may want to write a final draft
- once the final draft has been agreed, you can write the final summary.

Doing an effective summary

Doing a good summary requires the following skills and abilities. You need to be able to:

- **comprehend** the initial information, i.e. you will need to understand what the original text is about before you can make any real attempt at trying to summarise. Begin by reading it through twice – once to get the main idea and a second time stopping to look up words you don't understand and highlight areas where you need to get help
- **classify** the information, in other words, can you identify the related topics or points that are being made in the original text so that these can be put together as key points in the summary? Underline key words and phrases to highlight these points
- **analyse** the information, in other words, what are the implications of the text in the original? Is there a particular argument or point of view that is being developed and discussed? Try summarising the main argument or key point in a few sentences
- **evaluate** the information, i.e. can you identify the relative importance of points in the original text? Try listing the points in order of importance
- **select** the appropriate information, in other words, think about the most important points that are being made in the original – as these will need to be included in any summary. From your list of points select those to be included
- **present** the information using the appropriate format. This means choosing between one of the following:

  - a series of bullet or numbered points
  - a series of short paragraphs
  - representing the information in a graphical format, such as a table, chart or flow-diagram.

Student Activity

Read the following text entitled 'Examination Procedures'. The author of this text wants it to be summarised. Try to reduce the text, including the facts, but remove the headings so that it is continuous text. The numbered paragraphs under 'General Tips' should be indicated by the use of bullet points.

MEMORANDUM

TO:	Caroline Simpson (Administration Officer)
FROM:	Christine Edwards (Administration Assistant)
REF:	CE/CS/05
DATE:	25 January 19—

CONFIDENTIAL

REPORT ON INVESTIGATION INTO A4 PAPER WASTAGE IN THE ADMINISTRATION DEPARTMENT

1 INTRODUCTION

Before we closed for the Christmas break, you requested that I carry out some research into the increasing amount of paper wastage in the Administration Department. Your deadline for this report was 31 January 19—.

2 INFORMATION

The use of A4 paper within the department was investigated and the following sub-sections show where the majority of paper is used:

2.1 A4 paper used for printing purposes

All of the word processor operators were asked to complete a questionnaire which investigated the amount of wastage from this activity. The questionnaires were then analysed and it was found that at least one third of the paper which is supplied to the operators is wasted. This figure includes bond paper, company headed paper and memorandum paper. The word processor operators felt that they could economise on the amount of paper used, although most felt that they often missed errors when they were on-screen and only saw them when the hard copy was printed out.

2.2 A4 paper used for photocopying

All departmental staff who are issued with a code for the photocopier were interviewed. The majority of staff claimed that they wasted little or no paper when using the copier. A few of the staff felt that when they needed to enlarge or reduce original copies, then human error and size testing often meant that they had to have several attempts before the copy was accurate. All staff complained that the photocopier constantly jammed and that much paper was wasted because individual sheets continually 'concertinaed' and had to be destroyed.

3 CONCLUSIONS

The research I have carried out has proved that there is unnecessary waste of A4 paper in the Administration Department. The wastage is not restricted to only one area and it is unlikely that the situation will improve unless some action is taken. I therefore recommend the following:

3.1 Word processor staff should be encouraged to proofread all documents prior to printing. Some retraining may be necessary in order to facilitate this.

3.2 Electronic mail could be installed for use by the word processor operators so that hard copies do not have to be printed of internal mail.

3.3 The photocopier should either be serviced more regularly or, should funds allow, a replacement purchased. The copier is almost five years old now and this has some relevance to the jamming problem. Should the need arise it would be useful to consider hiring a machine.

Figure 5.1 An example memo-style short informal report

A decimal point referencing system would be laid out as follows, for example:

2 Information
    2.1 Canteen use investigated
    2.2 Students' comments from interviews held
    2.3 Canteen staff's comments from interviews held

Student Activity

You have been asked by your tutor to investigate the canteen facilities within the institution in which you are studying this course. You already know that many of the students are not particularly happy with the choice of meals provided and they also feel that the prices charged are too high. Your tutor wants to know if it is worth taking the matter to the Board of Governors. She asks you to carry out some interviews with the students and provide some feedback in the form of a memo-style informal report. You can use the example above to remind yourself how to use the decimal point referencing system. Make sure you include:

- subject
- introduction
- information
- conclusions

Your report should be word processed.

Simple notices

When an organisation needs to send information to a number of employees, a notice may be put on the staff notice-boards. Such messages may be formal or informal: perhaps a change to normal organisational procedures, or maybe a social event planned by the organisation's personnel department. Notices allow for the quick and easy transmission of information to a large number of people. Notice-boards at work can also be used by individuals wishing to inform other employees of items for sale, for example, or events planned. Nowadays electronic bulletin boards may also be found.

Notices are not always seen as a significant form of internal communication, when compared to reports and memos. However, they can be very important. Much information can be passed on via the staff notice-boards, such as social events, staff announcements, job vacancies etc. One of the main disadvantages of this method of communication is the fact that few organisations seem to nominate specific individuals to monitor the notice-boards, which can become very untidy and often display notices that are long out of date.

Different sorts of notices are required to convey different messages, but the following points need to be considered:

- size of paper – remember that most notice-boards are not very large, so don't use paper that will obscure other notices
- gaining attention – make the notice bold and clear enough to grab the attention of the passer-by
- passing on the message – don't make the notice too 'wordy'. State clearly and simply what you want the audience to read
- indicate any action required – if the reader needs to contact someone specific then ensure the person's name, department and telephone extension number are clear
- date the notice – so that the reader knows when it was first displayed
- sign the notice – so that the reader knows who to contact.

Design of notices

The effectiveness of a notice as a form of communication can be greatly increased by good design. An item of information that has been hastily handwritten or word-processed, all in the same font and in one continuous

DID YOU KNOW <u>JENNY BARNES</u> FROM
ADMINISTRATION IS LEAVING?

YES!!!!
ON FRIDAY OF NEXT WEEK!

FANCY COMING ALONG TO A FAREWELL DO?

THEN COME ALONG TO THE LOCAL AT 1700 HRS.

WE ARE ARRANGING A COLLECTION – SEE PHYLLIS
IN
ADMINISTRATION
ON EXTENSION 271

PHYLLIS GIBBS - ADMINISTRATION
13.6.1997

Figure 5.2 An example simple notice

paragraph, will have much less of an impact than the same information that has been laid out with care to attract the reader's attention.

Good use of design can include bullets (as in the paragraph above) to separate information, different sizes of text to draw attention to the important points, sub-heads to break up the text and graphics to make it interesting and add emphasis. Different typefaces or fonts, use of capital letters or **bold** text, can also add significance and will add to the general effect of the notice.

Student Activity

You work for the manager of a branch of a large retail organisation. You are expecting an important visitor. Prepare a notice for the staff notice-board which informs all employees of the forthcoming visit (you can decide the details yourself).

6

Marketing Department

■ Introduction

The main function of the marketing department is to try to identify customer requirements, and also to predict future customer needs as accurately as possible. The marketing department works very closely with the sales department and it is important that the two communicate well. But good communication with the research and design department and the production department is also an essential part of the marketing function.

■ Marketing communication

The marketing department will use several different forms of communication, both written and oral, in order to process information. The relevant types of information will include:

- sales information through invoices/order forms and letters and administration
- marketing research information (including data collection and analysis)
- customer care details (guarantees and warranties)
- information on sales promotions (such as special offers)
- the planning and monitoring of advertising
- support services information.

The nature of the marketing department means it is necessary to maintain high standards of effective communication in correspondence with customers. Both oral and written communication will be used to try to persuade potential customers to buy from their organisation and to encourage existing customers to remain loyal. We will look now at the key features of persuasive communication.

■ Persuasive communication

Persuasive communication can be used by any department or individual within an organisation in order to convince or influence someone to make a certain decision. It is usually the marketing department which will use this method of communication to convince or influence customers to make the decision to buy the organisation's products or services. Key words which are often associated with persuasive communication include:

- convincing
- motivating
- influencing
- advertising
- selling
- lobbying
- promoting.

Advertisements

In our everyday lives we are swamped by advertisements which try to persuade us to buy particular products. On radio and television, in newspapers and magazines, and on billboards and bus-shelters, adverts use persuasive communication to convince us, for example, that this particular washing powder is the best you can buy and that type of car is the fastest/safest/ smartest. A range of similar words can often be seen in such adverts. For example: *new* and *improved* are frequently related to washing powder or cleaning products, *delicious* and *healthy* applies to all kinds of food, *exciting*, *special* and *unique* can be found in adverts for all kinds of products, from cars and holidays to clothes and financial products. See what examples you can find for yourself.

Student Activity – Use of English

Concentrate now on your own ability to use appropriate words when attempting to persuade someone to do something. Write a list of typical words you would use if you wanted your friend to make a visit somewhere with you.

Communication techniques

Most managers will use persuasive communication techniques in order to motivate their staff. Such techniques will also be used by different departments in organisations for a variety of reasons. The following list shows some of the areas where this specific form of communication may be used:

- by the marketing department in advertising (in advertisements, posters, circular letters, sponsorship etc.)
- by the public relations department (in press releases, newsletters, letters to customers and clients)
- by the sales department (in direct selling, sales letters, promotional campaigns, conferences, exhibitions and trade fairs)
- by all managers (in communications with senior managers in order to obtain acceptance of a decision, in communications with junior managers in order to motivate and reassure).

Student Activity

Apart from the examples given above, for what other reasons would an organisation use persuasive communication? Write your own list and then compare to those of the rest of your group and discuss.

Before any persuasive communication can be successful, it is important that the organisation understands certain things about their target audience. Such features would include:

- outlooks and attitudes, which could vary with age or cultural background
- experience – particularly when considering the use of persuasive communication to sell computers and other forms of technology, for instance
- interests – even the most persuasive communication could not convince someone who had no interest in the relevant subject
- role and responsibilities – it would be a waste of time and effort trying to persuade someone to buy something if that person did not have any need for the item or the authority to place an order
- the relationship between the writer/speaker and the recipient – the style used in the communication may change drastically, depending upon the nature of the relationship between the two.

Student Activity

Taking a step further in the use of persuasion, you are now going to persuade your friend to make that visit with you (page 59). Carry out the following:

- in pairs, choose a venue for the visit. Your partner should listen carefully to your attempts at persuasion. After you have made all the arguments for your partner to go along with you, you should change roles and let the other person try to persuade you.

How good were you at persuasion? Give yourself a mark out of 10. What steps could you take to improve these skills?

Persuasive communication in marketing

In the marketing department, persuasive communication would be used in order to attempt to influence the purchasing decisions of the target audience or target market. The art of advertising is to find the right balance between what the organisation can offer and what the customer really wants or needs. Organisations use advertising to try to close the deal. Essentially, the marketing department would use persuasive communication in order to:

- launch a new product or service
- maintain or improve their current market position
- update a product or service
- maintain and improve customer awareness
- support sales campaigns
- promote corporate image.

Oral communication

When considering persuasive communication in oral form, the job of the sales representative springs to mind. As an employee, a sales rep. has to make a living out of selling something to someone else and so persuasive communication skills will be of vital importance if this is to be successful. What makes a good salesperson? The following list gives an indication of what is required:

- first impressions are important – the seller should be well-groomed and smartly but not fussily dressed
- knowledge – the seller should have a good knowledge about the product or service and be well informed about the organisation itself
- rapport – the seller should be at ease with other people and able to establish and maintain a good relationship with them
- ability to sell – the seller must be able to persuade customers that the product or service is right for them. A salesperson will do this by:
  - maintaining the rapport with the customer
  - establishing an interest in the product or service
  - explaining the major benefits of the product or service
  - overcoming any objections or answering any questions about the product
  - closing the sale.

This method of selling is discussed in more detail on page 65.

Written communication

Organisations, particularly the marketing department, use circular letters, press releases, sales letters, leaflets, advertisements and posters in order to communicate with their customers and potential customers to try to persuade them to purchase their products or services. We look at these different aspects of persuasive communication throughout the remainder of this chapter.

■ Circular letters

Circular letters, standard letters and direct mail are often used for advertising purposes. They usually take the form of a basic word-processed letter which is merged using computer software with a datafile containing names and addresses. Such letters are not always personally addressed and they may simply refer to 'the occupier'. This is particularly true of circulars, as many thousands of these are distributed in a particular mail-shot.

Circulars have three main goals, which are to:

- create an impact by using a striking headline or picture
- encourage the reading of the letter by using appropriate language or announcing that the individual will receive a free gift, for example
- be memorable by using appropriate slogans in large type.

Student Activity

Imagine that you are working for an organisation which needs to contact several hundred prospective customers by means of a circular letter. You do not wish to spend a lot of money on postage and the letters will be hand-delivered with a free newspaper. The circular letter will use the following information:

- Your organisation is planning to expand the services it currently offers by providing a delivery service. At the moment it offers a sandwich take-away service, but the management feel that there is potential custom for having sandwiches delivered at lunch-times to the nearby offices.

Write your letter offering the new service. You can decide the name of the organisation yourself.

Circular letters are often used to inform potential or existing customers of a new development or proposed event. The marketing department would use this method of communication to inform hundreds of organisations or individuals about the same event or piece of newsworthy information.

Tear-off slips on circulars

Quite often, when a circular letter is sent out, a reply is required. The easiest way to get the recipients to reply is to include a tear-off slip with the letter which can be completed and returned to the sender. The tear-off portion should appear at the end of the letter and can be produced by typing a continuous line of hyphens from edge to edge of the paper. Alternatively, you could include a reply-paid card which must be completed. In either case, it is worth remembering that the reply form/card can become detached from the circular letter. It is therefore important to include the name and address of the sender on the reply form/card as well as enough room for completion of answers.

Student Activity

Imagine that your school or college is to hold a fête in July of next year. The proceeds from this event will go to the Children in Need appeal. Your group is very keen to contact as many people as possible before the end of term so that you can get willing helpers and ask for donations to the raffle and some of the stalls.

Having found out the names and addresses of those you will be writing to, you should produce a draft circular letter. Remember to mention the date of the fête, the venue and the reason for the event. State clearly what you want the organisations to do and don't forget to give them a contact name and telephone number. Your letter should be word processed.

OPENING OF NEW CUSTOMER SERVICE SHOWROOM

THURSDAY 10 OCTOBER 19—

Please return by 13 September 19— to:

        Mrs R Lewis
        Marketing Manager
        RBT Electrics
        Market Street
        BUXTON
        Derbyshire
        D4 5NT

I shall/shall not* be attending the opening of your new Customer Service Showroom
at 4.00 pm on Thursday 10 October.

Name   --

Position --

Company --

       ------------------------------------ Tel no. --------------------.

*Please delete where applicable

Figure 6.1 An example circular tear-off slip

Press releases

A press release could be used if the organisation is not just interested in informing particular target groups, but is far more concerned with persuading the public in general. Press releases would be used principally for the reasons given below:

- press relations – as detailed above, by attempting to place newsworthy stories in order to attract attention to the organisation, its products/services and brands
- product publicity – to coincide with product launches or relaunches (such as new packaging etc.)
- corporate communications – aimed at communicating both internally and externally regarding the progress and developments of the organisation
- lobbying – communicating the views and opinions of the organisation to decision-makers in business or government.

Press releases form the back-bone of the majority of public relations activities. They are useful in that they are relatively easy to produce in whatever form is required and they can be sent to the appropriate individuals in the media before the launch date of the product or activity which is the subject of the press release. Although there is no 'magic formula' in producing a press release that is guaranteed to have positive results every time, the following points should be considered:

- **embargo date**
This is a date printed at the top of the press release which states that the information contained should not be published before a certain date. This is to ensure that press releases sent out before the launch date of a new product, for example, are not leaked before all the other marketing communications are in place for the formal launch date of the product

- **headline**
This should concisely explain the nature of the press release, which ideally could be used directly by the media for their headline in the publication. Although the media may not use this heading, they will be able to base their own version on this

- **factual opening statement**
The first paragraph of the press release should be purely factual and should explain exactly what the 'news' is

- **facts**
The media will be interested in press releases which contain useful and interesting facts and figures. These should always be true and supportable

- **quotations**
The media will also be interested in being able to 'humanise' the story by having direct quotes from well-known individuals (where possible). Whilst the media has probably played an active role in the collection of the news story, this will help give the impression that they have actually interviewed someone in the course of news gathering. If an external individual is being quoted (such as an MP) then the organisation sending out the press release will have to ensure that they have obtained permission

- **closing paragraph**
This is often seen as the summation of the press release, but is the part of the information that can be omitted from the 'story' if the media cannot fit the whole of the press release into their publication.

Style

As with many forms of marketing communications, press releases have a number of conventions or styles. These include the following:

- if the press release goes over onto another page, the phrase *more follows* is included at the bottom of the first page

- if the press release does go over onto the next page, then the last two or three words of the first page are repeated on the next page
- at the end of the press release, the word *ends* is used to show that the press release is complete
- the organisation's name, address, telephone number, fax number and e-mail address should be placed at the end of the press release. A named individual should also be quoted so that the media knows who to contact for further information.

In order to make it as effective as possible, the following points should be considered when writing a press release:

- always be factual
- do not allow emotion to creep in
- stay impartial
- keep it newsworthy but do not exaggerate
- try to appeal to human interest
- do not be too statistical
- channel information to the appropriate area
- be as up-to-date as possible
- make sure the press release is produced professionally
- include all relevant information (names, addresses, telephone numbers etc).

Student Activity

Over the next week or so, try to collect as many press releases or company statements as possible. Once everyone in your group has collected a few, discuss their worth. Do you think they were well-presented and interesting? Grade them all from 1 to 5 and write a short paragraph about each. State why you thought they were particularly good or bad. How would you have improved on them?

■ Producing leaflets and advertisements

A good way to approach this task can be to consider the 'AIDA' technique

AIDA is an acronym, which stands for:

- Attention – you must get the attention of the reader
- Interest – you need to tell the audience something that appeals to them, to get their interest
- Desire – try to arouse a desire to buy, to try or to contact the writer
- Action – try to make the audience do something, in other words carry out the action that you want from them.

We will now consider some helpful guidelines to enable you to create advertisements/leaflets that will mirror these aspects of the AIDA technique. Remember that the average person is exposed to over 1500 promotional messages every day of the week – so there has to be something special about what you are trying to say to them. It is essential that you try to hold their attention otherwise vital parts of your message will be missed by the audience. The guidelines below primarily refer to the written word:

- try to put a promise in your headline
- offer a benefit or a solution to a problem
- try to appeal to the self-interest of the audience
- try to create visual images with words
- link the first sentence of the main text of the advertisement with the headline
- state facts – don't generalise
- remember that what you are saying may not be what the audience is currently wanting to hear
- try to be persuasive
- use 'you' as often as possible to get the audience involved, i.e. make it personal
- make the sentences and paragraphs short, but readable
- use sub-headings if necessary
- use everyday language, don't be too technical and avoid jargon
- avoid long words
- explain everything that the reader needs to know
- try to make the audience carry out the action you want
- if you have a reply section in the advertisement/leaflet, be as persuasive here as you have been elsewhere
- try to tell them that responding to your advertisement is in their best interests, make the response beneficial to them
- be very clear about how the audience can respond
- make it as easy as possible to carry out the actions that you are urging
- don't just tell them how to do it – tell them to do so now!

Headlines

We will now look at some of the points in this central set of guidelines in more detail, exploring what is meant by some of the terms and approaches. The headline, being the first thing that grabs the audience's attention, is the most important consideration. There are some key points to remember about headlines:

- make sure to put a promise into the headline. Research has shown that five times as many people read the headline than read the body of an advertisement. This is because the majority of headlines do not grab (and keep) the attention of the reader
- make sure that the audience has a reason to read on – what is in it for them?
- make sure that the headline is relevant to the audience
- don't try to be funny if you are not very good at it. Sometimes humour works, but in most cases the audience will not find it amusing or will be bored

- make sure that you don't exaggerate. Only use superlatives if they are really appropriate
- make sure that you create a strong visual image in the minds of the audience
- make sure that you only use everyday language
- never use words that are unnecessary. Every word should be vital so keep the headline brief
- try to persuade the reader to read on. The body copy will help persuade them to act
- never write an anonymous headline – use words such as 'you', 'your company', 'your home' and 'yourself'.

Body copy

The body copy of an advertisement is used to support the statements made in the headline and to expand upon the ideas/concepts that are part of the message. There are some key points to consider in writing effective body copy:

- remember to link the first sentence/paragraph with the headline
- if you have posed a question in the headline, make sure that you answer it immediately
- appeal to the self-interest of the reader
- focus on facts, features and benefits
- don't jump about – make the sentences and paragraphs flow together
- use language that the reader will understand
- be clear about what you say and try to be persuasive
- don't waste words – brevity is best
- repeat yourself only to reinforce a point
- only use short words (unless you are sure larger ones have a greater impact)
- make use of sub-headings and cross-headings
- make use of bold, italics and other typefaces
- like a letter, keep an idea contained within a sentence or a paragraph
- try to make sure that the audience can respond positively to the advertisement/leaflet.

Student Activity

Following on from the activity on page 62 you now need to produce an advertisement for your July fête. This will be placed in local shop windows, in your own school/college and in other local schools. Look back at the guidelines above, make sure you include everything important, and don't forget to check your spelling!

■ Newsletters

One way for an organisation to inform all of its employees of matters of interest is by issuing a newsletter. Some large organisations use newsletters to contact all their members of staff, where they have different branches around the UK.

These newsletters can include both formal and informal information. For example, a newsletter may state the fact that a director is retiring or that one of the staff has recently had a baby.

Student Activity

In pairs, find out if your school or college produces a newsletter for its staff or whether the student union provides a regular newsletter for its student members. What information do they contain? How often are they issued? Do people read them? Present your findings in a memorandum to your tutor.

■ Invitations

Informal and formal invitations may be sent or received by organisations. When these are being issued in bulk, they are normally printed by a specialist company and simply prepared for postage within the organisation. The formal invitation may take the form of a letter or card. An invitation will usually contain the following information:

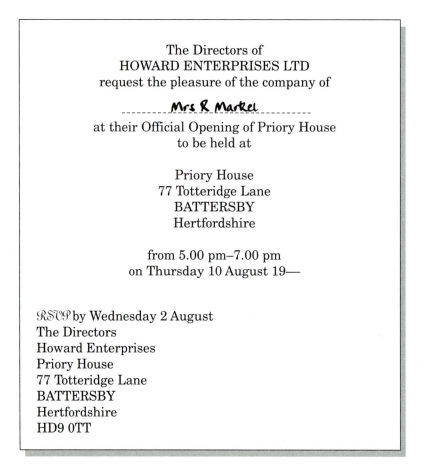

The Directors of
HOWARD ENTERPRISES LTD
request the pleasure of the company of

_____ Mrs R Markel _____

at their Official Opening of Priory House
to be held at

Priory House
77 Totteridge Lane
BATTERSBY
Hertfordshire

from 5.00 pm–7.00 pm
on Thursday 10 August 19—

RSVP by Wednesday 2 August
The Directors
Howard Enterprises
Priory House
77 Totteridge Lane
BATTERSBY
Hertfordshire
HD9 0TT

Figure 6.2 An example formal letter of invitation

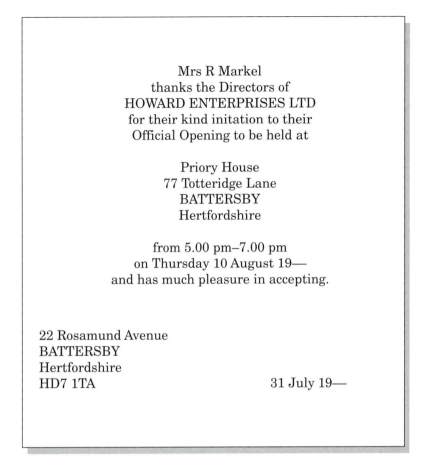

Mrs R Markel
thanks the Directors of
HOWARD ENTERPRISES LTD
for their kind initation to their
Official Opening to be held at

Priory House
77 Totteridge Lane
BATTERSBY
Hertfordshire

from 5.00 pm–7.00 pm
on Thursday 10 August 19—
and has much pleasure in accepting.

22 Rosamund Avenue
BATTERSBY
Hertfordshire
HD7 1TA   31 July 19—

Figure 6.3 An example acceptance of a formal invitation

- address of the person sending out the invitation
- date the invitation is sent out
- names of the people acting as host at the event
- date of the event
- location/venue of the event
- time of the event
- reason for the event
- RSVP – this acronym is a request for a reply and is taken from the French phrase 'respondez s'il vous plâit'. Sometimes a deadline for replies is also given.

When replying to a formal invitation, the acceptance or refusal can be prepared in a similar way to the invitation. However, it is polite to give a reason if an invitation is refused.

Student Activity

You now need to produce an invitation to someone in your local town who can open the fête. Write a list of all possible individuals. You could include local councillors, or maybe you have a TV or sports personality living locally? Produce the invitation using a word processor.

Student Activity

You work for the manager of a large retail organisation. You are expecting an important visitor (choose a TV or film star, politician or music personality). Produce an invitation which is to be sent to several key customers who your manager wishes to be present when the important visitor arrives. Remember to include all the details and to proof-read your work.

Production, Research and Development Department

7

■ Production

The production department is involved in all functions of the organisation which are concerned with producing products or services.

The production department of any large manufacturing organisation would be responsible for carrying out the following activities:

- manufacture the products
- monitor wastage and relevant costs of production
- assist in the designing of machinery
- assist in the writing or buying-in of computer software to contribute to the production processes
- control the production rate
- monitor and control the quality of products
- monitor the production processes of competitors.

■ Communication needs

The production department will need to communicate with several other departments within the organisation, including:

- sales
- marketing
- purchasing
- research and development
- accounts
- human resources
- administration
- warehousing
- distribution.

Student Activity

Using the list above, compile a table which gives possible reasons why the production department might need to communicate with each of the departments mentioned.

The production department would also communicate on a regular basis with suppliers. It would not, however, tend to communicate regularly with customers and clients. The other departments of the organisation would make and maintain this contact and filter the information through to the production department.

The nature of the communication involved, both within and to and from the production department, means it is unlikely that this particular department

The procedure for sending a telex message is as follows:

- have ready the telex number of the recipient. This will be done in the same way as for the fax machine, but using the telex directory
- prepare the text of the telex – typed on the telex machine
- make contact with the recipient by keying in the telex number
- obtain confirmatory answerback code from the recipient
- provide identification in the form of the answerback code of the sender
- despatch the telex.

```
Author: Jane Rogers at Howards
Date: 25/09/97
Priority: Normal
TO: Richard Matthews at Howards
TO: Karen Andrews at PLC
CC: David Smith at Howards
Subject: New Computers


------------------------------ Message Contents ------------------------------

You will be pleased to know that the Board has approved the
installation of new updated computers. The installation will take
place on 24 October 1997 and up-to-date software will be installed
at the same time. There will be some inevitable disruption during
the installation, but this will be kept to the minimum.
```

Figure 7.2 An example e-mail print-out

Electronic mail

Electronic mail or e-mail offers all of the facilities provided by fax and telex, but is paperless. Electronic mail offers the additional benefit that messages can be stored when the destination terminal is busy. Electronic mail systems offer a variety of common features, which include:

- terminals to prepare and store messages
- communication link with other work stations within the network
- central controlling computer
- directory of addresses
- central mailbox
- system which dates the message
- function to note that the message has been received by the addressee
- facility to multiple-address so that all members of a particular working group are sent the message simultaneously
- prioritising system so that messages can be identified as important or routine

- storage facility in order to keep in the memory those messages that have not yet been received
- compatibility with existing equipment and computer systems.

However, e-mail offers a number of advantages in relation to other forms of communication, including:

- savings on stationery and paper costs
- saving on telephone costs
- rapid transmission
- integration with other systems, such as the computer system used in that organisation
- recording of all transmissions so that accurate costings may be obtained
- allowing employees to tele-work, i.e. they can be working at home with a computer but still have access to all the information in the office using e-mail via a modem link
- allowing addressees to look through their electronic mail when they have the time.

Electronic mail documents may also be printed out, however, if a permanent copy of something is needed.

Student Activity

If an organisation had fax, telex and electronic mail available, say which would be the best method of communication to use for the following:

- notice to be read by all managers within the organisation
- urgent order to one of the suppliers
- confirmation letter to a supplier based overseas
- production figures in the form of graphs to be sent to head office.

■ Designing simple forms

One of a production administrator's tasks may be to design a form for the specific recording of information or for ordering purposes. There are several key factors to consider when designing a form:

- make a rough copy first so that you can check the layout and general appearance
- make sure that you have included all the necessary headings
- ensure that the heading are not ambiguous, but are clear for the user
- take care to leave sufficient space under each of the headings (some will require just one line, others will require several)
- ask a colleague to check the form to pick up any errors you may have missed
- think carefully about the look of the form – it is better to redo it initially than to use it every day knowing you could have done a better job.

- set out the facts clearly
- be relevant
- be polite
- state that you require a favourable response, explaining what this is.

Planning the letter

When writing a letter of complaint it is important to structure the letter carefully and to state exactly what you want your complaint to achieve. For example, if you were writing to a shop to complain about a faulty new appliance you would need to explain that you wanted it mended or replaced. In some instances, you might want your money back rather than a replacement. Throughout the letter you should use a polite and controlled tone, not allowing annoyance or frustration to get in the way of the message.

Imagine, for example, that you had bought a new television and it failed to work properly the next day, when you had invited some friends round to watch a film with you. When writing your letter you would first explain why you were writing and give details of the TV, when and where you had bought it, the price, model number and so on. You would need to start another paragraph to say what went wrong with the television and how it happened. A third paragraph could explain the inconvenience and annoyance caused when you and your friends gathered to watch the film and the TV did not work. Then the final paragraph would set out what you wanted to happen next, i.e. a service engineer to call as soon as possible to mend the TV or to exchange it for another one.

When writing a letter of complaint you should be able to see a distinct structure – a beginning, middle and end – with each paragraph being used to make a particular point.

Student Activity

Imagine that you had bought an electric coffee machine as a present for a member of your family. The first time it was used, the machine pumped boiling coffee out of the top and it was only because you were able to turn it off quickly that no-one was scalded. Write a letter of complaint to the manager of the shop where you bought the machine.

In response to the letter of complaint, the organisation may have to write a letter of apology. In addition to the apology, this may involve the following:

- financial compensation
- an offer to replace the goods
- an undertaking that the situation will not arise again
- an undertaking that an individual within the organisation has been disciplined.

If the organisation discovers that the complaint is without justification then, in order to maintain goodwill, a token offer may be made. Whatever the circumstances, justified or unjustified, letters relating to customer complaints should be carefully put together. They should always use restrained language, such as, 'Please be assured that this situation will not arise again'. All letters of complaint should be dealt with promptly, but sometimes enquiries may need to be undertaken before the complaint can be addressed.

Student Activity

Imagine that you have purchased a toy for your niece/nephew's birthday. On the special day, when the child opens the present, you find that it is faulty. Write a letter of complaint to the manufacturer.

8

Human Resources Department

■ Introduction

The human resources or personnel department is responsible for the management of all employees in an organisation, in particular the well-being of all staff. This is important not only from a human viewpoint, to keep the workforce happy, but so that all employees can work to the best of their abilities.

■ Functions

The human resources department has a number of important functions, including:

- the 'hiring and firing' of employees – this includes all the procedures and policies necessary to comply with the various articles of employment legislation
- the education and training of employees, which should allow staff to develop in order to improve the overall effectiveness of the organisation as well as on an individual basis
- staff welfare, this would include the various measures to assist employees with any problems (both inside and outside work), the provision of social and other facilities etc.
- industrial relations – this would include dealing with employees in the case of disputes or misunderstandings between them and the management. This may involve the representatives of employees (probably a trade union) or the negotiations and resolution of the problem may be carried out on an individual basis.

■ Recruitment

As already mentioned, selection and recruitment are a major function of any human resources department. In order to ensure that this process operates in an efficient and effective way, the human resources department would carry out a number of activities.

Job descriptions and person specifications

A job description details the main responsibilities and tasks of a job, as well as the chain of command. A person specification, on the other hand, identifies the skills and personal qualities required. The main purpose of job descriptions and person specifications is to ensure that the individual matches a series of desired criteria. It is clearly necessary, when recruiting someone, to fill the particular needs of the organisation. These fall into three main categories:

- accurately matching potential employees with existing vacancies
- making sure that the job design relates to the overall business objectives of the organisation
- being prepared to provide additional training and development if required.

The **job title** given to the tasks, duties and responsibilities involved is the first item to appear on the job description and should be as specific as possible. If the job involves some form of supervisory or managerial responsibility, then it is normal for the job title to be suffixed by the word 'supervisor' or 'manager'.

The job description should clearly state the level of the job in the overall structure of the organisation. It is usual for the job holder to know precisely to whom he or she is accountable and for whom he or she is responsible.

The job description must also clearly state the **responsibilities** entailed. These may simply detail the specific job tasks and duties, but may also relate to supervisory or managerial functions.

Student Activity

Working on your own, choose an advertisement from a local newspaper and compose a job description for that job. You should be careful to choose an advertisement which contains the maximum amount of information. If the advertisement does not contain all the details necessary to complete the job description, then you should make reasonable assumptions about the hidden requirements of the job.

A **person specification** covers the main characteristics required to do the job. These will include:

- current achievements – qualifications, driving licence, if applicable, and previous experience
- aptitudes of the individual – depending upon the job, this may include social skills, listening and communication skills or legible handwriting
- the person's intelligence
- the person's interests – any relevant sports or leisure activities, particularly any positions of responsibility held in relation to these
- the personal circumstances of the individual – these will include domestic situation and personal relationships and the availability and willingness of the individual to work overtime or at weekends
- the physical make-up of the individual, for example how the person looks and whether he or she can speak clearly.

Student Activity

In pairs, using a clerical assistant's job as your example, prepare a list of criteria which you would consider to be either essential, desirable or required. This list should be word processed.

Advertising

An advertisement for a job can be placed in either the local or national press, or in trade journals or magazines. Some organisations are able to produce 'camera ready' advertisements which can be placed directly into the newspapers. This means that, using a desk-top publishing program, the organisation will produce an advertisement of the correct size and dimensions to conform with the size of the advertising space that has been purchased. Usually someone in the human resources department will be responsible for liaising with the local press and will know who to contact to book advertising space and how much notice needs to be given. In other cases, the organisation will book the advertising space and the newspaper's design staff will create the advertisement. This is a more expensive way of placing advertisements in the newspaper, but is useful for those organisations which do not have the skills or equipment to carry out the necessary design work.

As an alternative to placing an advertisement in the newspapers, the organisation may use the services offered either by the local Job Centre or a private employment agency. In such cases, the human resources department will need to liaise with these outside agencies to ensure that they know exactly what type of candidate they are looking for. Usually this would involve sending a copy of the job description to the agency or the Job Centre, which will then sort through the records of individuals registered with them to see if there are any suitable candidates readily available. Failing this, they will advertise on behalf of the organisation and carry out the initial selection and short-listing functions for them.

Application forms

An application form will be sent to all potential candidates. Most organisations will have a pro-forma application form that can be used for all jobs: this may have been designed by the organisation or can be obtained 'off the peg' from a number of organisations that prepare and sell standard forms. At this stage, the potential candidates will have contacted the organisation either by phone, in person or in writing and will have requested a copy of the job description and the application form. The organisation will also, in most cases, send out any other relevant information regarding the nature of the business to potential candidates.

Timing is very important and the organisation needs to ensure that there are enough application forms and supporting information available for the probable demand from potential applicants. Because the application form is a standard form (that is always stocked by the human resources department) and the other information is of a general nature and can be collected from the relevant department of the organisation, the only additional problem is that of the job description and the person specification. Since these are not long documents, a small stock could be copied initially and then added to if the demand for information is high.

APPLICATION FOR EMPLOYMENT

Name	Address
	Phone No.

Date of birth Age	Position applied for
Marital status	Names and ages of children

Health give details	Driving licence YES/NO Endorsements YES/NO (give full details)
Are you a registered disabled person YES/NO if yes give registration no.	

Education History Schools Colleges/Further Education Other	Qualifications obtained:

Previous employment begin with present or last employer and work backwards.

Name of Employer	Position held	From - To	Give full details of job	Rate of Pay

Please give any other information which you feel to be relevant to your application for employment i.e. Sports, hobbies, ambitions, interests etc.

References please give details of two referees one of whom should be your last or current employer. These references will not be taken up without your permission.

Name Address	Name Address

For office use only

Applicant engaged Starting date	YES / NO	Rejection letter sent Date	YES / NO
Engagement letter sent Date	YES / NO	General comments on Candidate	
Personnel File opened	YES / NO		
References applied for (Date)	YES / NO		

Figure 8.1 An example standard application form

In order to receive as many completed application forms as possible, the requests for information should be responded to quickly. In most cases, the human resources department will be 'geared up' to expect a number of requests and may allocate one or more individuals to cope with these for a few days. The size of the demand for application forms and information will depend upon the nature of the post and the popularity of the newspapers in which the advertisement featured.

Short-listing

Short-listing can be a complex process which may involve a number of individuals at different levels of the organisation. It should take place at the earliest possible opportunity after the closing date of the applications. The short-listing process can be carried out by a member of the human resources department, probably in consultation with either the human resources manager or the future manager of the post-holder. There will always be a number of applications that are deficient in some way, such as those that have been poorly completed, very messy or are otherwise unacceptable. These applications can, in most cases, be discarded before any serious attempt to tackle the short-listing takes place. Each of the applications, or CVs and covering letters, will need to be looked at carefully in order to compare them with the person specification and the job description. Ideally, a short-list should not number more than about five or six potential candidates. This is not always possible and there may be some disagreement regarding the choice of short-listed candidates. In these cases, it is often better to extend the short-list by one or two candidates.

Interviews

In Chapter 10 we look in some detail at the interview techniques for potential candidates when applying for a job. For the organisation, the first key communication issue is to decide who will be included on the interview panel. A good starting point would be those who have already been involved in the short-listing process, perhaps supported by another manager or supervisor from a different part of the organisation.

Briefing the interview panel before the interviews take place is the responsibility of the human resources department. At the very least, the panel will need to be supplied with the person specification and the job description so that they know exactly who they are looking for. Ideally, the interview panel should have been given the opportunity to prepare a series of standard questions that will be used in all of the interviews and they should all have been given the chance to look at the application forms or CVs before the interview date.

At the interview itself, the candidate will be trying to give the best impression possible to the interview panel, which in turn will be attempting to ensure that they question and test the interviewee in a fair, but firm manner, in order to find out as much about the candidate as possible. Interviews are conducted in a number of different ways, from the informal interview (which may be a more casual and friendly exchange of information) to very formal interviews, where the candidate is faced with a large interview panel and is tested and questioned rigorously for a considerable period of time. The length of the interview will depend upon many different criteria, including the importance of the post and the amount of time which the interviewers can afford to devote to the process.

When all of the interviews have been carried out, the interviewer will need some time to consider the candidates and to try to agree which one is the most suitable for the post. Sometimes first and second interviews are needed to ensure that as much information as possible is gained from the candidates for the job.

Making an offer

A successful candidate will be offered the job and those who were unsuccessful informed of the outcome either by letter or by telephone. Sometimes the job is offered to the successful candidate on the day of the interview, in which case this task will be carried out by the panel. Usually the human resources department will handle the communication and this can be carried out face-to-face, by telephone or in writing.

It is usually the human resources department which also contacts the unsuccessful candidates (see below). Some organisations simply send out standard letters, whilst others prefer to give the unsuccessful candidates some feedback regarding their performance at interview. Usually, when letters are sent, the human resources department will invite the unsuccessful candidate to contact them for feedback if they wish. When the unsuccessful candidates are given the news by telephone, it is possible to offer some comments from the notes made by the panel. In all cases, the organisation will need to ensure that the human resources department passes on travel and other expenses claims from all of the candidates to the accounts department in order to reimburse them at the earliest opportunity.

References

Taking up the references of the successful candidate is often the final step before confirming an appointment. It is common practice that the human resources department sends out a letter and/or form requesting that the referee makes some comment on the candidate's abilities, character, quality and performance. The request for the reference often takes the form of a standard letter with the candidate's name clearly visible so that the referee knows exactly what is required. Provided the reference(s) are suitable and positive, then the candidate's appointment will be confirmed. Quite often, this stage is just a formality that has to be completed and it is unlikely that the successful candidate will fail at this late stage of the process.

Rejection letters

As mentioned earlier, it is usually the human resources department which will have to write to unsuccessful candidates to inform them that they have not been called for interview or have failed to obtain the post they applied for. Obviously, this type of letter will require some tact. The organisation would not wish to upset the individual concerned. The person writing the rejection letter will not want to be unkind when they say 'no' to the candidate, whether this is to someone who has applied for the job externally, or to an individual who had hoped for promotion of some kind.

When writing a tactful rejection letter, it is important to remember the following:

- introduce the subject of the letter in the opening paragraph. Say why you are writing and what you are responding to
- use the second paragraph to state that the application has been unsuccessful
- follow on with a further paragraph which explains the bad news, but try to bring out some positive points here. Perhaps you could say that the candidate came over very well at interview, or that the organisation will be in contact in the future if another post becomes available – but only say things that are true and do not give the candidate false hope
- close the letter by saying something positive, perhaps by wishing the candidate good luck in his or her future career.

■ Contract of employment

It is a legal requirement that all employees new to an organisation are given a written contract of employment. It is also expected that such contracts are issued within 13 weeks of starting the job. A contract of employment lists the rights and responsibilities of both the employer and employee.

A contract of employment is like any other contract; it gives both parties rights as well as obligations. The contract identifies formally what was agreed during the interview or selection process. Usually, a contract of employment will state the following commitments:

- the employer will pay wages/salaries
- the employer will provide work
- the employer will pay any reasonable losses or expenses incurred by the employee in the course of his/her work
- the employer will provide a reference if required by the employee
- the employer will provide safe working conditions and practices
- the employer will not act in such a way as to breach the trust and confidence given by the employee
- the employer will provide necessary information relating to the employee's work, pay, conditions and opportunities
- the employer will always act in good faith towards the employee.

■ Appraisal interviews

Assessing the work performance of individuals within an organisation is the role of the personnel department. But, on a day-to-day basis, performance appraisal may be the concern of line managers and supervisors. Appraisal interviews should be a two-way process of feedback between the manager and employee. The aim is to improve performance through a joint problem-solving approach. The interview should be conducted in a pleasant and positive way throughout. The following hints and tips may be useful to managers when conducting appraisals:

- give enough notice to the employee to allow time for preparation, possibly including a self-development review form
- choose a quiet room for the meeting and allow enough time for each interview
- prepare carefully, looking at the employee's previous appraisal and subsequent performance
- look at previous targets at the start of the interview and praise any good performance
- ask questions about what has gone well and what has not gone well, enquiring about the causes and admitting responsibility where necessary
- summarise what has been agreed at the end of the interview and allow the employee to read the appraisal documentation.

Employees need to make the most of appraisal interviews and should:

- prepare well before the interview, making notes of past performance results and anticipating any difficult questions
- not be too modest about strengths or put too much emphasis on weaknesses. Good work may sometimes go unnoticed but mistakes are not usually missed
- be clear about what support is required for future work, such as training, resources or time to reach targets. This may be the opportunity to secure training and development to support longer-term career aims
- remember that an organised and positive approach will help to make the interview more pleasant and less stressful.

Purposes of appraisal

The main purposes of appraisal are to:

- identify employee weaknesses
- identify employee strengths
- determine salary increases (in some organisations, however, appraisals are not linked to salary reviews)
- determine who deserves promotion
- aid internal communication processes within the organisation
- determine staff development needs.

After the appraisal, the employee and appraiser will draw up an action plan which will cover all aspects of the appraisal interview. This will form the basis of the next appraisal interview. There will be an opportunity at this meeting for the employee to respond and offer evidence that issues identified in the previous appraisal interview as unsatisfactory have been rectified.

■ Group discussions

It is usually the responsibility of the human resources department to form a staff association made up of representatives from all different parts of the organisation to discuss a range of company issues. Standing as a representative for your department will involve taking part in group discussions.

Student Activity

As a group, in the role of the staff committee at your college, consider what action you could take if it was reported that the student canteen area was to close down due to lack of money. It has been proposed that no refreshments will be available anywhere on site at the college. After the discussion, make notes on how any differences of opinion within the group were handled.

When you take part in group discussions it can be very demanding to perform the roles of both speaker and listener. However, there are certain strategies to help individuals put themselves forward and make their views known in group discussions. These include:

■ a good preparation for all meetings/discussions, including notes on what you want to say
■ if there is no notice of the discussion, wait a few minutes to gather your ideas and then put forward your view
■ make statements clear, brief and concise, establishing the reason for speaking and developing points in a sensible order
■ do not speak just for the sake of saying something but make all contributions relevant
■ invite others to respond.

When taking part in group discussions, listening skills will play just as important a role as speaking skills. **Active listening** means allowing others to put forward their own views so that in discussions everyone will listen and respond to each person's contributions. It involves hearing and understanding what others are saying – blocking out distractions, checking if anything is unclear and perhaps summarising in your own words at the end what has been said and getting confirmation from the speaker that this is correct.

Non-verbal communication (or body language) also plays an important part in discussions. Someone who is using active listening skills is likely to display the following positive non-verbal signals:

■ positive body positions, e.g. sitting forward slightly
■ open hand and body movements (i.e. not crossing arms or legs)
■ good eye-contact with the speaker (but not staring)

■ attentive facial expression and supportive gestures, e.g. nodding or smiling when appropriate.

Such examples of good non-verbal communication apply equally to speakers, for example, maintaining good eye contact but not staring at your listeners and so on.

Team building

Good and effective working relationships are enhanced when you can get on well with other people. You are more likely to gain the cooperation of others if you possess at least some of the following characteristics:

■ positive attitude
■ friendly and helpful personality
■ efficient and business-like approach
■ sympathetic and tactful behaviour when necessary.

In a well-functioning team there should be a comfortable and relaxed atmosphere, in which discussion is open and extensive and everyone knows what they are doing. Decisions are reached by consensus and disagreements are resolved as a group. Criticism should be free and frank but related to the task and not personalities. In such a group, trust and cooperation are paramount. However, it can take a lot of work to get a group to this level of effectiveness.

9

Accounts Department

■ Introduction

The accounts or finance department in an organisation will need to have excellent systems of communication and administration in order to fulfil the department's function of assisting in planning, decision-making and financial control. These systems must be capable of recording financial information, storing records and having them available for inspection when required, and providing data for financial reports.

■ Recording financial information

As mentioned above, one of the functions of the accounts department is to record financial information in an efficient and effective manner, making it possible to retrieve and analyse this information as and when required.

When any financial transaction takes place, it is essential that a record is kept by the organisation. These records have to be stored safely and securely, and must be easily accessible and up-to-date. Financial transactions are recorded for the following reasons:

- there is evidence that the transaction has taken place – it is not sensible to rely on the memory of those people involved in the transaction. The records can then be checked at a later date
- the accounts department can pay the bills and collect any money owed to the organisation
- the accounts department has a record of the transactions in order to produce the annual accounts for the organisation
- the business performance of the organisation can be monitored – the accounts department will want to work out the profit or loss figures to get an idea of how well the organisation is doing
- a public limited company is legally bound to keep records so that it can inform its shareholders as to how the organisation is performing
- the VAT can only be assessed by the Customs and Excise Office if it has access to the organisation's records of financial transactions
- the income tax (for small businesses) and the corporation tax (for limited companies) can only be assessed by the Inland Revenue if it has access to the organisation's records of financial transactions.

Documentation

The Accounts department uses a range of business documentation to undertake financial transactions with customers and staff. The most common types of documents are listed below.

Invoice

An invoice is an official request for payment by an organisation. The details which appear on an invoice may include the following:

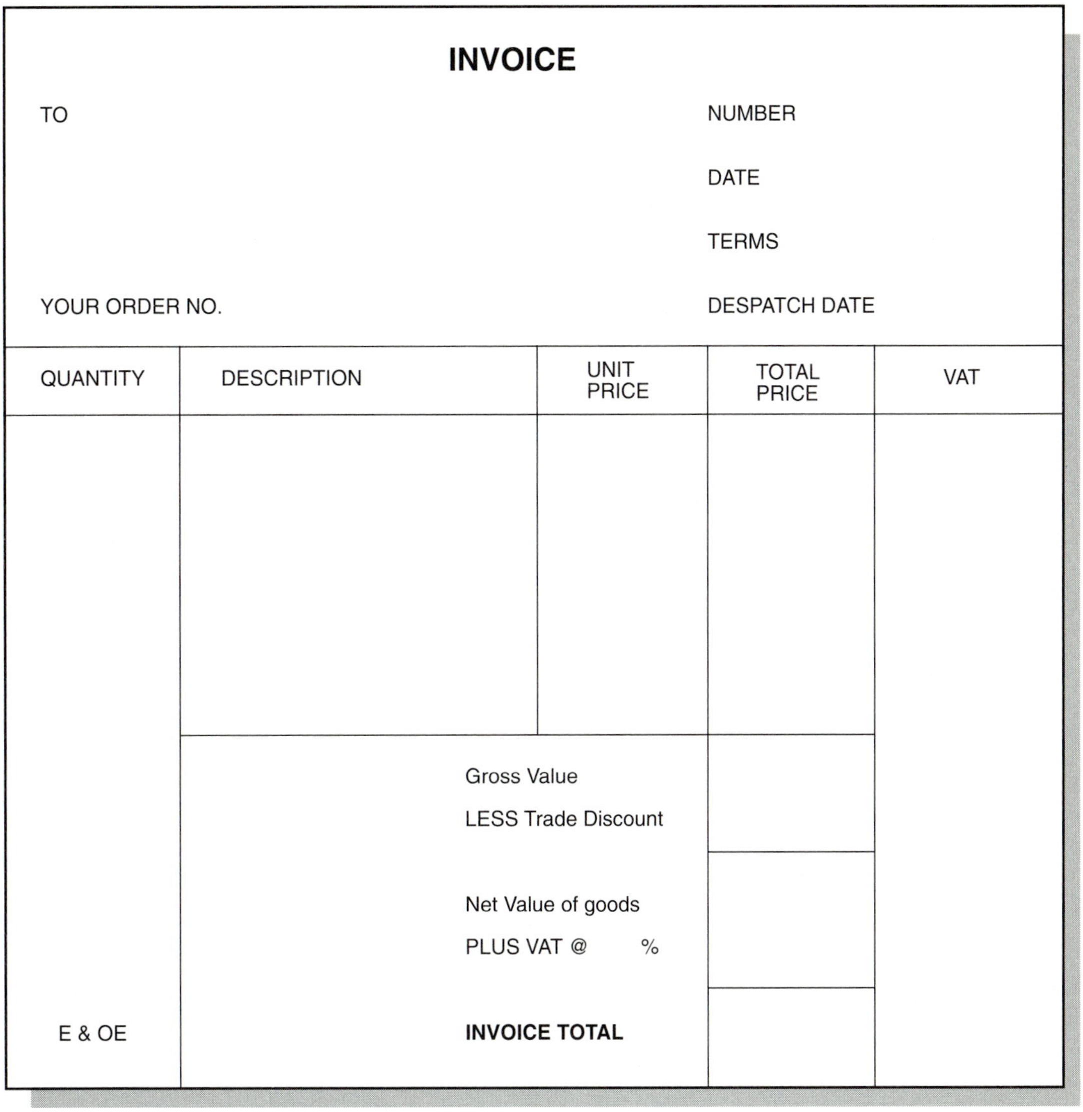

Figure 9.1 An example blank invoice

- details of the goods or services supplied
- individual prices of those goods or services (the invoice may include many individual or multiple goods or services supplied)
- VAT that has been charged on the goods or the services (if applicable)
- total amount that is owed by the receiver of the invoice
- terms of the trade (i.e. when the amount outstanding is due to be paid to the sender of the invoice)
- name, address, telephone (etc.) and legal identity of the sender
- name, address, telephone (etc.) and legal identity of the receiver of the invoice
- VAT registration number of the sender
- invoice number
- date of the sale or the tax point of the invoice
- receiver's purchase order number

- account number allotted to the receiver of the invoice by the sender.
- the abbreviations E & OE (errors and omissions excepted) which means that the sender of the invoice can correct mistakes on the invoice at a later date.

Credit notes

Credit notes are issued in order to rectify an omission or an error which has led to the overcharging of the customer by the supplier. There are a number of different instances that could cause this to happen, for instance the incorrect completion of an invoice by the accounts department of the supplier, if the customer has been over-supplied (perhaps duplicate deliveries have been made in error) or if the customer has had to return some goods included on an invoice as a result of them being unsuitable, damaged or not acceptable for some reason.

CREDIT NOTE

TO

NUMBER

DATE

ORDER NUMBER

INVOICE NUMBER

QUANTITY	DESCRIPTION	UNIT PRICE	TOTAL PRICE	VAT
	Gross Value of Goods			
	LESS Trade Discount			
	Net Value of Goods			
	PLUS VAT @ %			
	CREDIT NOTE TOTAL			

Figure 9.2   An example blank credit note

Most of the details on a credit note will be very similar to those on an invoice. For this reason, most credit notes are issued in red in order to distinguish them from invoices. The credit note is prepared by the supplier and sent to the customer.

Statements of account

Once a month, usually at the end of each month, the supplying organisation will send out a statement of account to each of its customers. This statement will list the transactions that have taken place between the two companies. It will show the totals of each of the sales invoices sent to the customer, plus any payments made by the customer during the month. The balance shown at the end of the statement is the amount still to be paid by the customer to the supplying organisation.

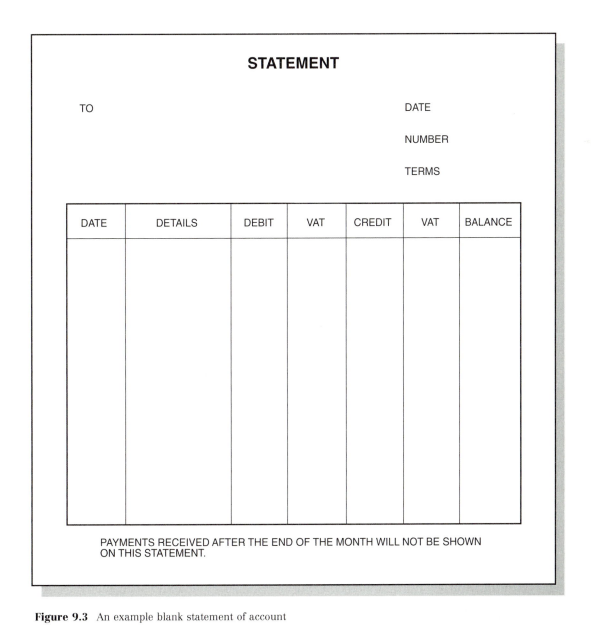

STATEMENT

TO

DATE

NUMBER

TERMS

DATE	DETAILS	DEBIT	VAT	CREDIT	VAT	BALANCE

PAYMENTS RECEIVED AFTER THE END OF THE MONTH WILL NOT BE SHOWN ON THIS STATEMENT.

Figure 9.3 An example blank statement of account

Pay slips

As an employee, one of the most important and interesting documents that an accounts department deals with from your point of view will be your pay slip! Wages and salaries can be paid in a variety of different ways – by cash in a pay packet each week, by cheque sent to your home either weekly or monthly, or by bank transfer (usually monthly) to your own bank account. Whichever way you receive your money, you will still receive a pay slip, issued by the accounts department of the organisation. The following will be itemised:

- your name and sometimes your address
- your pay reference number
- the pay period for which you are being paid
- your tax code and the amount which has been deducted, plus the total amount deducted to date
- your national insurance number and the amount that has been deducted, plus the total amount deducted to date
- your contributions towards a pension scheme
- any voluntary contributions you make which are deducted from your wage/salary
- your bank details, if you are being paid by bank transfer.

PAY ADVICE

N. I. Number	Tax code	Basis	Year	Period	Pay No	Pay Centre

GROSS PAY	STANDARD DEDUCTIONS		VOLUNTARY DEDUCTIONS		NET PAY
Code			Code		
Total Gross Pay			Total Deductions		

Hours worked		TOTALS TO DATE	VOL. DEDUCTIONS	
Normal	Overtime			
			Code	Balance Owed

Figure 9.4 An example blank pay advice slip

Petty cash

Another routine duty of the account department may be the monitoring of the petty cash supplies. It may be that the organisation or office keeps a small amount of cash for use on a casual basis. Anyone requesting petty cash must complete a Petty Cash Voucher detailing what the money is required for.

PETTY CASH VOUCHER

	Folio ....
	Date ....

FOR WHAT REQUIRED	AMOUNT	
	£	p

Signature: ....

Authorised by: ....

Figure 9.5 An example blank petty cash voucher

Expenses claims

If it is company policy for an organisation to reimburse its employees for any expenses incurred whilst travelling on behalf of the company, then the logging of these expenses is a requirement of the accounts department. An Expenses Claim Form would be completed as a one-off exercise if it were an unusual trip, or as a matter of routine if the employee travels regularly for the organisation.

EXPENSES CLAIM FORM

NAME: .... DEPARTMENT: .... CODE: ....

BANK ACCOUNT NUMBER: .... SORT CODE: ....

DATE	PARTICULARS OF JOURNEY	CAR MILEAGE	PUBLIC TRANSPORT	CAR HIRE	HOTEL DETAILS	MEALS	VAT	TOTAL

I testify that these expenses have been incurred during the course of my normal business activities.

Signed: .... Date: ....

Authorised by: .... Status: ....

Figure 9.6 An example blank expenses claim form

Student Activity

You work within the accounts department of your organisation. Some communication problems have been encountered again and again over recent months. You have been asked to compile a memorandum which is to be sent to all other departments. The following problems have been encountered:

1 It has been increasingly apparent that not all staff are familiar with the procedure for requesting petty cash. Some members of staff have not had the documents authorised before making their requests.

2 Items which have been ordered over the telephone have not always appeared on order forms, despite the fact that they have been despatched to customers. Some members of staff are not writing the orders down as they are received on the telephone.

3 Invoices are taking too long to be despatched to customers. This is causing cash flow problems within the organisation. At present the average time to despatch an invoice to a customer is seven working days. This must be reduced to no more than four.

You should identify the departments to whom the memorandum must be sent and issue recommendations to each of them in order to solve the problems.

▪ Oral presentations

It is often the role of individuals working within the accounts department to present financial plans to the Board of Directors or senior management. Obviously, this will require extensive knowledge about the financial strengths and weaknesses of the organisation, but it will also involve the use of several important communication skills. We intend in this section to look at the communication skills involved.

The key to making a successful presentation is good preparation. You have to make sure that your material is well organised and that you can deliver it to the best of your ability. The idea of giving a presentation may seem rather daunting at first but it will help if you prepare well and use some of the techniques outlined below.

Preparation

The following steps will help towards good preparation of your presentation:

▪ find out how long your presentation is expected to last
▪ research your audience – will they be familiar with the subject matter of your presentation? This will help you decide on how much background information you will need to provide and whether you can use jargon or not

- should the presentation be formal, semi-formal or informal in approach?
- find out about the venue and consider the practical details – are there enough chairs, is there an overhead projector (and perhaps blinds or curtains as well) if required, can you rearrange the furniture if necessary, and so on
- write up all your notes, to include everything you want to say
- work out ways of illustrating your presentation, perhaps using posters, overhead transparencies, hand-outs at the end and so on.

Organisation

Once you have gathered all your material you will need to plan your talk. It is important to make sure you have a definite beginning, middle and end. For example:

- introduce yourself and explain what your presentation is about
- expand on your subject, making one point at a time and illustrating each point with an example or a visual aid
- summarise your main points again in the conclusion
- thank the audience and ask if there are any questions.

When you make your presentation you will not be able to look through pages of notes so it is a good idea to write brief notes on cards as prompts. On each card there could be one key phrase, followed perhaps by three points to expand what you are saying.

At this stage you will need to create your overhead transparencies and any other visual aids. Then, when you have organised all your material, you should have a 'practice run' in front of a colleague or friend to gain some honest criticism of your presentation and to see how long it is. You should also think about what you are going to wear on the day – a smart appearance and good grooming are vital.

Delivery

Being well-prepared will help make your presentation a success. Make sure that you are at the venue in plenty of time before it is due to start. You can then check the final details of the room, check that the overhead projector is working and so on, and still have a few minutes in which to gather your thoughts.

When you are delivering your presentation, try to remember some of the following points:

- aim to look confident and smile at your audience – be enthusiastic!
- make sure that all of your audience can hear you – and ask them if you are unsure
- make eye contact with your audience but do not stare at only one individual – look around
- keep your body language open and welcoming, and try to avoid any irritating gestures
- speak slowly and clearly, using short words and sentences

- remember that varying your tone of voice and pace of delivery will add interest
- allow for some pauses, to let important points sink in – try not to speak non-stop.

At the end of most presentations there will be a question and answer session and it is important to allow enough time for this. You should also:

- check to make sure you have heard questions correctly if they seem unclear
- keep answers brief and relevant
- be honest – if you do not know the answer to a question admit it and say you will find out.

Student Activity

Working in pairs, imagine that the two of you are about to embark on opening a small business of your own. You can decide on the type of business yourselves. One of your major considerations is the acquisition of appropriate finance for this venture.

You have made an appointment with your local bank manager (your tutor could play this role) and you have to present a valid argument as to why the bank should lend you the money to start up your business. Spend some time before the oral presentation in getting your facts and figures straight and then try to convince your tutor that your venture is a feasible one.

■ Using charts, tables and graphs

Statistical diagrams are often of use to the accounts department (and other parts of an organisation) as they can display data in a clear and unambiguous form. They are therefore a powerful communication tool, capable of displaying complex information in an easily comprehensible form.

Pictograms

Pictograms are perhaps the simplest way of displaying data. The creator of the pictogram has to choose a picture which suits the data (i.e. money could be represented by a £ sign etc.). Each picture used in the pictogram represents a specified value of that data, so for example, if the total value of the data is £100,000, then each £ sign could represent £10,000 and therefore ten £ signs would be used. (see Figure 9.7, opposite).

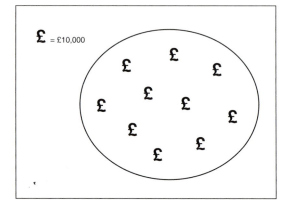

Figure 9.7 A pictogram

Graphs

In general, graphs have a number of rules and conventions attached to the manner in which they are constructed:

- the horizontal line is known as the x-axis and the vertical line is known as the y-axis
- each axis should have a clear scale which allows the information to be displayed clearly on the graph (this means that you should take advantage of all of the space available on the page)
- a line graph should have the points joined together, whereas a scatter graph should not
- always ensure that you give the graph a title and, if possible, state the source of the data that has been used to create the graph.

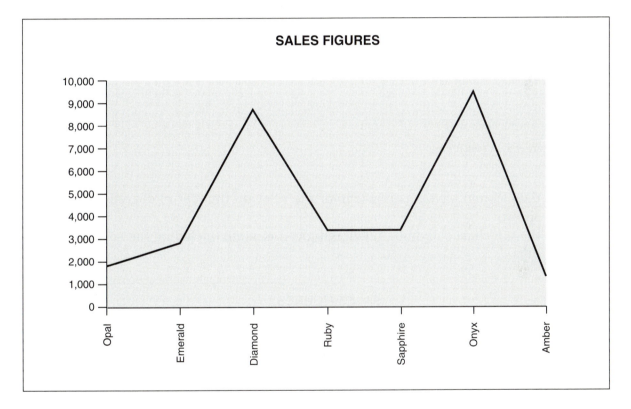

Figure 9.8 A line graph

Pie charts

A different form of graphic representation of data is the pie chart. A pie chart is always shown in a circle with each slice showing the portion of the whole it represents. There are a number of features which can be associated with the construction of a pie chart:

- the circle consists of 360 degrees
- each of the 'slices' or sections of the pie which you allocate to a value of the

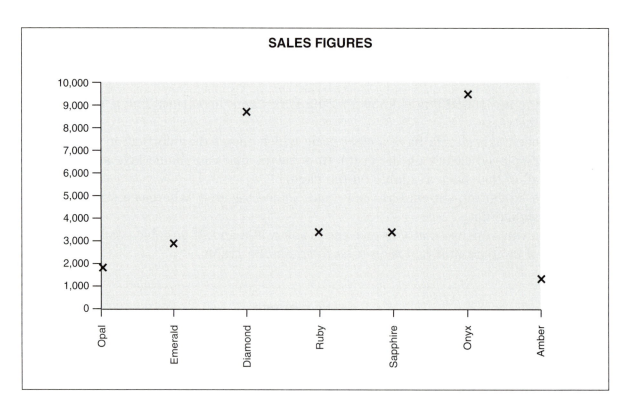

Figure 9.9 A scatter graph

data should have a percentage or the relevant number of degrees clearly shown

■ the pie chart should be titled and given a name (including the source of the data).

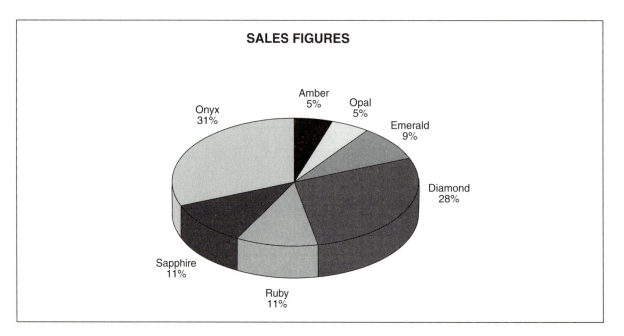

Figure 9.10 A pie chart

Below is an example of how to calculate the number of degrees that should be attached to a particular value:

Average number of employees per day	
Monday	30
Tuesday	30
Wednesday	35
Thursday	40
Friday	35
Saturday	30

First, add up the total number of employees. This comes to 200.

Now calculate the number of degrees that should be attached to each section of the pie chart:

Monday $\dfrac{30}{200} \times 360 = 54$

Tuesday $\dfrac{30}{200} \times 360 = 54$

Wednesday $\dfrac{35}{200} \times 360 = 63$

Thursday $\dfrac{40}{200} \times 360 = 72$

Friday $\dfrac{35}{200} \times 360 = 63$

Saturday $\dfrac{30}{200} \times 360 = 54$

Note that the far right-hand column (i.e. number of degrees) adds up to 360. These figures can be shown as percentages on a pie chart by dividing each figure by 360 and then multiply by 100, e.g. $54 \div 360 \times 100 = 15\%$

Histograms or bar charts

An alternative to a line graph is a bar chart. However, a bar chart uses bars instead of continuous lines. The bars can be shown vertically or horizontally.

Tables

Using tables of figures is an integral part of the work in any accounts department as they are used to summarise various data in a compact and clearly labelled format. Normally, tables are constructed in such a way as to be figure-only versions of what many graphs represent.

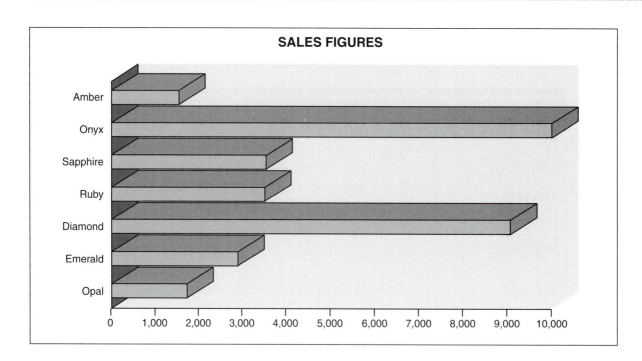

Figure 9.11   A bar chart or histogram

Student Activity

Using the charts given in Figures 9.8 to 9.11 above, identify the following:

- which of the organisation's products has the most sales?
- which or the organisation's products has the least sales?

Which type of graph or chart did you find most useful for extracting this information?

Student Activity

You have been given a mass of information and figures to sort out for a presentation to your colleagues. The information includes your organisation's sales figures for the past year, sales figures by region and total sales over the past five years. You have to decide which format to use for presenting the following information:

a   The proportion of total sales for each geographical region.
b   The volume of sales each month for the last financial year.
c   The trend in sales figures over the past five years.

Compare your choices with others in your group and discuss why you decided on those formats.

All of the above can be used nowadays in conjunction with a computer software package. The information or data has simply to be input into a spreadsheet package and then the computer will give you a choice of ways in which this information can be displayed and ultimately printed out as hard copy.

This method of communicating information has some advantages over the spoken or written word, including the following:

- much more detail can be expressed
- the audience is likely to be more interested in a chart or diagram than a long, complicated explanation
- the information, once stored on computer, can be easily updated should the need arise
- charts and diagrams can be printed onto an overhead transparency sheet or onto a slide negative, in order that the information can be given to large numbers of individuals at a presentation.

10

Applying for a job

■ Introduction

Applying for a job involves a number of different stages. First, you have to look for a suitable job advertisement (or, alternatively, find an organisation where you would like to work in order to write and offer your services). An application form will be requested and then filled in correctly, or you may need to write a letter of application and send in your CV (curriculum vitae). If successful, you will be asked to attend an interview to find out whether you are suitable for the job (and also whether it is suitable for you!). If you are then leaving one job to do another, you will have to write a letter of resignation to your current employer. In this chapter we will look at all these different stages, examining the communication needs of each.

■ Looking for a job

It is usually necessary to use a variety of sources to find a job which suits a person's skills, experience and aspirations. These sources will include:

- national daily press
- professional journals
- trade journals
- television
- radio
- local daily/weekly newspapers
- free newspapers
- career centres
- job centres
- private employment agencies
- 'word of mouth' or personal contacts
- self advertisement.

When responding to an advertisement, an applicant needs to consider the following questions:

- am I in a position to apply for this post – do I have the qualifications and skills required? (This may include the preparation of a curriculum vitae)
- is it the right sort of job for someone with my experience?
- what do I already know or what can I find out about the organisation offering the post?
- does the organisation have a good reputation?
- how does it treat its staff?
- are there any opportunities for personal development?
- are there good promotion prospects?
- do I need to send a letter of application to obtain additional information about the post?

Applying for a job may involve the following:

- obtaining, then filling in an application form
- writing a letter of application
- researching the organisation
- preparing a curriculum vitae (CV).

Student Activity

In preparation for designing your own CV, make a list of your skills and qualifications, and any work experience you may have done. Include part-time jobs and also any other achievements, such as the Duke of Edinburgh Award Scheme. You will need correct details of school and college, when you were there and so on, so it is worth including these under separate headings also.

■ Letters of application

An organisation advertising a job may require applicants to write a letter of application. The basic rules about writing a letter of application are as follows:

- clearly state in the first paragraph that you are applying for a particular post
- state in this first paragraph where you saw the advertisement for the vacancy
- indicate any enclosures, such as an application form or CV
- use the letter of application to summarise your major strengths (as would be detailed in an application form)
- stress your suitability for the post
- be enthusiastic
- keep the letter of application short – no more than one side of A4
- use the correct layout for a business letter
- make sure that the letter is formal and uses the correct salutations and complimentary close (i.e. Dear sir – Yours faithfully or Dear Mr Smith – Yours sincerely)
- state that you are available for interview and say when
- say when you are able to start the job
- take a photocopy of the letter
- make sure that any examination certificates required have been photocopied – do not risk sending the originals.

Usually a business letter would be typed or word-processed but many recruitment advisers recommend that this letter of application is handwritten. If you choose to handwrite your letter make sure it is neat and tidy, with no crossings out or smudges. If necessary, do several copies and choose the best.

■ Application forms

Rather than sending a letter of application you might have to fill in a standard application form. An application form may appear to be rather daunting at first, but if you follow the guidelines given below it will probably be easier than you think to fill in the details. The guidelines are:

- photocopy the original and always fill in a rough copy first
- spend some time thinking about the more tricky questions – come back to them later if necessary
- make sure that you have spelt everything correctly and used the right grammar
- when filling in personal details, make sure that your answers are neat and legible. This first part of the application form can make a valuable first impression on the reader
- if asked whether you have any specific skills, emphasise the ones which you think are particularly useful for the post
- in mentioning your achievements, try to identify something you have done which can show personal development or initiative on your part
- make sure that you know the correct details of the examining board and date of all examinations and qualifications you are doing
- give some thought to the inevitable open-ended questions, such as 'Why have you applied for this position?'. In order to answer these questions you will need to have carefully read the details about the jobs, including any skills or competences required
- choose your referees with care and make sure that they are well-respected members of the community.

Before you write anything on the original application form, make sure that you have answered all of the following questions:

- have I answered everything?
- are there any periods of time in my life which are unaccounted for?
- have I actually answered the questions, or have I simply stated something?
- is my approach positive?
- do I think that the reader will gain a favourable impression of me?
- do I need to attach any proof of qualifications or perhaps a photograph?
- have I been honest and can I substantiate everything I have claimed?

Filling in an application form

We will now look at the details of filling in the different sections of an application form. Remember, if you are filling in the form by hand (i.e. not typing it) you should always use black ink (so that the form can be photocopied) and write in capitals where required.

Name

This should normally take the form of the surname in capitals first, then the forenames (i.e. first names) afterwards. The full name should be included. The name should also indicate the title desired, such as Mr, Mrs, Ms, Dr and Rev.

Date of birth
This can be given as either a simple numerical date of birth, such as 24.4.78, or in full – 24 April 1978. The day should always be first, followed by the month and the year.

Address and telephone number
The address should be given in full, with the number, street, town, county and full postcode. It should be presented in the following way:

> House number/street
> TOWN (in capitals)
> County
> POSTCODE (in capitals)

The telephone number should be in full, with the area code first (in brackets), followed by a space, then the rest of the number. Alternative telephone numbers where the applicant may be reached should also be included, together with details of when to use which number. For example:

> (01941) 662243   (9.00 to 5.00)
> (01941) 644320   (evenings)

Employment
The employment history section can be difficult to get right as there is so much to include. Some basic rules apply, however:

- always work backwards in time (unless directed otherwise on the application form). In other words, give the latest (last) employer first and then the previous one, and so on, so your first employer is at the bottom of the list
- give the correct name of employer in full, along with the address
- if required to state tasks, job role and duties – be brief (you may not have much space). Always mention the details which are most relevant to the job you are applying for
- give dates (as appropriate), being as accurate as possible
- if there is a gap in the employment record (in terms of the chronological order) make sure that the potential employer realises that you were doing something else (for example, education, training, looking for work etc.)
- you may be asked for your current salary details, as well as a reason or reasons for leaving your present employment. Always be truthful – a potential employer may check these statements.

Education and training
Again, the reverse chronological order system applies here. Start with the last education and training undertaken and work backwards in time. Give accurate dates and clearly and fully state the institution(s) that you attended. If the institution has changed its name or status, try to make sure that you give the new name/address and state what it was 'formerly' called. Do not put your qualifications here in detail as this is usually covered under the next section of the application form.

Qualifications

There is rarely enough space to include all qualifications here. If necessary use a separate sheet and mark it 'qualifications'. Put your qualifications in reverse chronological order, along with:

- grades obtained (including special grades)
- examining board.

Also detail your 'pending' results and the date by which you expect to have attained them.

Other relevant achievements

Be brief in this section and do not include irrelevant or inappropriate achievements. An employer may not be interested in the fact that you have a 25-metre swimming certificate (unless you have applied for a job in a swimming pool!).

Useful achievements include:

- duties/responsibilities at school or college
- special awards (such as Duke of Edinburgh Award Scheme)
- any press coverage of special events you have been involved in.

Interests

An employer does not want to be told that your main leisure occupation is 'drinking with my mates' – even if it is! 'Socialising' covers a multitude of sins, but again, be brief, and try to come up with interests that may be of interest to the employer and relevant to the job. It is important to be truthful, so be careful not to say things like, 'I enjoy reading eighteenth-century literature' unless you do – as the employer may ask you about it!

References

Someone who provides you with a reference is known as a referee. Employers like to take up references to be sure that what you have said in your job application is correct. Referees should always include your present (or last) employer, or school/college principal/head teacher, as appropriate. Do not use direct family members for your referees. If you can find a person of status or responsibility (such as a doctor or lawyer) willing to be your referee, then take the offer up. In most cases, two referees will be sufficient, but occasionally three are asked for. You should always ask your referees for their permission before putting their names on a form or CV.

■ Curriculum vitae

The curriculum vitae or CV is usually sent when the organisation asks you to 'send full details'. The purpose of a CV (which means 'course of life') is to summarise your career so far, i.e. all your personal details and past experience. The way in which CVs are produced is very much down to the individual and a CV should be designed to match the specifications of the job applied for. The

---

CURRICULUM VITAE

Name

Address

Telephone no.   (home)
                       (work)

Date of birth

Marital status

Nationality

EDUCATION
DATES   SCHOOL/COLLEGE/UNIVERSITY   COURSE

Qualifications
DATES   SUBJECT AND LEVEL   GRADES

EMPLOYMENT HISTORY
DATES   EMPLOYER   POSITION/DUTIES

Training

Other information
(e.g. driving licence, voluntary work)

LEISURE INTERESTS

REFEREES

1   2

Figure 10.1 An example of the headings used in a CV

style of the CV should be concise and clear. It should include only the relevant facts and figures and should be in note format. See Figure 10.1 for an example of all the headings which should be included on a CV. Remind yourself of some of the rules when filling in details about your personal details and past experience by turning back to the earlier section on filling in application forms. A CV should certainly be word processed, for the following reasons:

- it will look neat and well-presented
- it can be updated regularly
- it can be adapted to suit different job applications.

The content of the CV will obviously depend upon the job you are applying for. But you should ensure that:

- it is not longer than two sides of A4 (preferably only one)
- it is a summary of your education and career so far
- it is clear and well presented
- the tone is positive and optimistic throughout.

You should keep a copy of your CV and read it before you have an interview.

Student Activity

Thinking more about your own curriculum vitae and the need to obtain referees for job applications, write a list of people you feel you could approach to provide a reference for you.

■ Interviews

The interview has two basic purposes:

1 to help the employer choose the employee
2 to help the employee choose the right organisation to work for.

Being an interviewer

It is important to structure the interview in such a way as to find out the most about the applicant and for the applicant to find out as much about the organisation as possible. All essential information should be on hand and the interviewer should pre-prepare questions and answers to potential questions from the interviewee. We will now look at the good practice recommended for interviewers.

Opening the interview

A few minutes should be spent first in putting the applicant at ease. It may be a good idea to open the interview with some friendly questions about the interviewee's interests. Normally, it is advisable to help set the scene by considering the following aspects of an interview:

- **perceptions** – make sure that the physical surroundings are private. There should be no interruptions or phone calls. Think about the position of the chairs and tables
- **social** – make sure that the candidate is greeted properly and is offered tea/coffee etc
- **facts** – help the candidate understand the purpose and content of the interview, explain how it is going to be structured.

Asking questions

There are many techniques that can be used when asking candidates questions at interviews. Some of the more successful techniques for interviewers include the following:

- ask open questions which require the candidate to give more than a simple *yes* or *no* response. Remember that you want to know what the candidate is really like
- you can use silence as a way of encouraging an interviewee to say more
- do not talk for more than about 30 per cent of the interview time
- try to be flexible. If you have a pre-prepared list of questions, do not stick slavishly to them
- take notes, but do not be too interested in getting things down on paper at the expense of listening to what the candidate is saying
- make sure that the candidate is willing to accept the job, if offered.

Remember that open questions are often best since there is no pre-determined or 'right' answer.

Asking follow-on questions

Follow-on questions can often reveal more than the initial enquiry. If you want to get the most out of the interviewee, it is not advisable to leap into asking another question before the interviewee has had a chance to finish speaking. Therefore try to use follow-on questions to help the interviewee develop an answer.

It is a good idea to find out if the candidate wants to ask anything. Use this time also to encourage the candidate to tell you about any qualities which match the job that may not already have been addressed or included on the application form.

Student Activity

Below are some questions commonly used by interviewers. They are designed to encourage candidates to reveal a little more about themselves and are all examples of open questions. Read the questions carefully:

1 What aspects of your work do you find the easiest and the most difficult?
2 What has been your greatest success to date?
3 What are your strengths and weaknesses?
4 Which aspects of your work do you enjoy the most and which do you enjoy the least?
5 How will you feel about having to move home if you are offered this job?
6 What is the most attractive feature of this job which encouraged you to apply?
7 What strengths do you feel you could bring to the job?

In pairs, try these questions out on one another in response to a job advertisement. How clear and believable are the answers? Do you think that you are prepared for questions such as these? Keep a written record of your responses.

Follow-on questions should be phrased in such a way as to clarify, amplify or expand on matters that have been touched upon in initial questioning.

Non-verbal communication

The spoken language is not the only useful form of communication. Body language or non-verbal communication is a powerful tool in interviews. It can either support what you are saying or undermine it, particularly if the body language is inappropriate.

Good body language for an interviewer could include the following:

- always face the interviewee
- do not sit directly opposite (this can seem too confrontational)
- try to be natural
- try to have a receptive (relaxed) posture
- try to lean slightly towards the interviewee (this shows an interest in the person and what he or she is saying)
- try to match the body language of the interviewee (but be careful not to look as if you are imitating it!)
- dress in your usual work clothes
- behave as you would do normally
- try not to be threatening
- use direct eye contact when appropriate.

Many of these points would also be useful to interviewees.

Student Activity

Try out some body language techniques with a partner. In turns try to convey the following emotions without saying anything:

- surprise
- pleasure
- frustration
- boredom
- anger
- nervousness
- alertness
- interest
- attention
- friendship

How do your interpretations differ from those of your partner?

Closing the interview

By the end of the interview the candidate should feel that there has been plenty of time to respond to all of the questions, leaving the interviewer in no doubt about any of the details or meanings. The interviewer will normally say something like, 'We will need to finish shortly' and then begin to summarise what has been said. The interviewee also needs a last chance to add to or clarify anything.

Full close should include a handshake and thanks from the interviewer. The interviewee should know when to expect a decision or what is the next stage of the selection process (a test or second interview, for example). It is important to leave the candidate at ease and ensure that an on-going relationship has been established.

Being an interviewee

A candidate for a job knows that he or she has got to the interview stage in the recruitment process when a letter from the organisation arrives with details of the date and time of the interview. This is good news for a job applicant and means it is now time to begin preparations for the interview phase.

In this section we will consider the nature of these preparations and also aspects of interview technique, including:

- assertiveness
- body language
- framing questions
- listening skills.

Preparing for an interview

The potential interviewee will quickly reply to the organisation with a letter or telephone call accepting the interview date. As advised earlier, candidates should keep photocopies of the application documents. Now is the time to re-read all of this information and begin to draft a list of possible questions which might be asked. It is wise to find out as much as possible about the organisation prior to the interview. Specifically, this should include:

- nature of the organisation
- products and services of the organisation
- markets in which the organisation is involved
- typical customer of the organisation
- obvious competitors of the organisation.

This information may be obtained from company reports, articles in the press, libraries or, if the candidate is particularly keen, by trying to obtain a tour of the organisation (if appropriate).

The final phases of preparation for the interview should include the following:

- working out the most reliable and direct route to the organisation and testing this route beforehand, if possible
- listening to the radio on the day of the interview to find out if there are any transport problems
- choosing suitable clothes to wear at the interview
- allowing enough travelling time to allow for any possible delays
- in the event of arriving early, the candidate should not go into the building more than 10 to 15 minutes before the expected arrival time.

Showing confidence

The issue of confidence and assertiveness needs to be carefully considered. Interviewees must attempt to get their point of view across at all costs, but should not be aggressive. When speaking, interviewees should remember the following points:

- while replying to a question, look at the person asking the question
- be positive and optimistic in response
- never lie or 'stretch the truth'
- always answer the question that has been asked
- if something is not clear, ask for the question to be repeated.

Listening to questions

It is important for an interviewee to develop speaking skills in the interview situation, but it is also essential to make full use of all listening skills. For a good communicator, listening is just as important as speaking – perhaps more so. If you are going to be a good listener, you should remember the following:

- concentrate on what is being said
- avoid distractions
- prevent the mind from wandering
- repeat key words or phrases to yourself

- look at the speaker's non-verbal communication, i.e. gestures and posture
- be alert for pauses in the speaker's speech
- be ready to respond when required but do not interrupt
- give the speaker feedback, perhaps by nodding
- be alert for opportunities to give personal responses.

Student Activity

Can you think of six questions that you would wish to ask at an interview? Why would these questions be necessary? Discuss this in pairs.

Responding to questions

When preparing for an interview, remember that it is an information-gathering exercise for both you and the interviewer. To give short or non-committal answers to questions will not leave a good impression. Above all, you should not be frightened to say what you believe. The important thing to remember is that you should only talk about things that you know about.

The interviewer will, usually, attempt to frame questions in such a way as to get particular responses from you. These question types include the following:

- **trust questions** – where the interviewer will ask something that indicates faith in your judgement. A typical question might be, 'There is a big problem with sickness at the moment and it causes difficulties in getting orders out to customers in time, what do you think we should do about it?'. Be careful here not to make any assumptions, you may not know the organisation well enough to be able to give any detailed advice. Try to be general, but never say, 'I don't know'.
- **clarifying questions** – in these types of question the interviewer will ask whether you understand something fully. An example of this would be, 'You know that we use a computerised stock control system, do you think that you could operate it?' Be truthful again; if you have experience in computers, then this is fine, but do not say you know how to use a system that you do not really understand
- **empathising questions** – these deal with the problems and concerns that the candidate may have. A typical question would be, 'How would you feel about taking a rather junior position in the organisation?'
- **open questions** – remember that these do not have a right or wrong answer. Such questions give the candidate the fullest opportunity to reflect and give depth to an answer.

Another set of questions that you may find require a slightly different approach. These include the following:

- **criticisms** – where the interviewer may make a statement which expresses some doubt about your experience or ability to do the job. In this case, a simple response which illustrates that you are capable is enough. If you do not have the required qualities, then do not attempt to bluff. Honesty is, as they say, the best policy

- **testing** – these questions attempt to determine whether the candidate is capable of making a right or wrong decision regarding a certain question. The interviewer may have pre-conceived ideas about the correct answer. It is difficult to double guess what will be required. Some clues may be given, by accident, in the body language of the interviewer. However, a clear and sincere response is a good one, regardless of whether the interviewer thinks your answer is correct

- **leading** – these questions attempt to get the candidate to respond in the manner that the interviewer expects. In most cases, it may be a good idea to go along with the interviewer's intentions. If the candidate does not respond in the way expected, this may stop any further questions in this line of enquiry

- **closed** – again, as mentioned earlier, the interviewer may use this type of question when requiring a quick or simple response. Normally, the expected response is either *yes* or *no*. In other cases, the candidate may be required to give a date, time, or other basic response. These questions do not give the candidate the opportunity to talk further about the subject.

Asking questions

We have already mentioned the sort of questions which may be asked by the interviewer or an interview panel. A candidate who is preparing questions for an interview should take the following into account:

- ensure that the questions are clear and have been understood
- ensure that the questions are not repeating what has already been said
- the questions should not be sarcastic or cynical in tone
- the interviewee should not try to be funny
- questions should be asked at the appropriate time
- the interviewee should never butt-in or interrupt an interviewer.

Being clear and concise

The general rule is to make statements that are unambiguous and easy to understand. In this respect, regardless of the nature of the question, you should take your time and consider what you are saying. Try to say all of what you want to say and do not leave statements 'up in the air' or unsubstantiated. Always remember that the interview time is restricted. The interviewer has a list of questions and areas of enquiry to cover. It is the candidate's responsibility, and in their own best interests, to make sure that there is no room for misunderstanding. The interviewer should always be left with the impression that the candidate has fully addressed the questions and given a satisfactory response. Remember that it is better to give a clear and concise response than try to 'waffle' about a subject that you are unsure about. A good interviewer will notice this and will try to cut short the candidate who is wasting or 'playing for' time.

Student Activity

Working in pairs, you are to carry out a role play of an interview. You must take it in turns to be the interviewer and interviewee, allowing 10 to 15 minutes for each interview. You should decide first the details of the organisation, the position that is vacant and any characteristics of the interviewer and interview that you think are relevant.

When you have finished your role plays, come together in your group to discuss your experiences. Was it harder to be the interviewer or the candidate? What insights have you gained? How could these help you when you next have an interview?

Mock examination papers

The mock examination papers which follow will help you to prepare for your final examination – Communication in Business Stage II. There are five written practice papers and five oral practice assignments.

■ Written practice papers

You should allow two and a half hours to complete each of the written papers under exam conditions. All the questions should be attempted in the order in which they appear. The mark allocation is given for each question and this should be taken into account when planning your work.

Information obtained from one question may be used in answering another and dictionaries/spell-checkers may be used.

■ Oral practice assignments

The oral practice papers which appear in this book prepare you for the oral assignments which make up part of the Communication in Business Stage II award. These practice papers provide you with a scenario to simulate with the help of your tutor who has a specific role to play.

■ Written Practice Paper 1

General information applicable to all questions

(Information obtained from one question may be used in answering another.)

Following the departure of the personal assistant to the Managing Director of Emma Levy Advertising Associates, your role has been temporarily expanded to cover her work too. Having worked as an administrative assistant for Emma, you know how she likes to do things and see this as an opportunity to try to gain the personal assistant's post. In the meantime, you must show that you are capable of doing all of the work that has been given to you. Emma is not in the office very often as she spends a great deal of her time with the clients and in liaison with the various sub-contractors.

Emma is not exactly demanding, but the last personal assistant only survived the role for three months; in fact, in the past two years Emma has had four personal assistants. The advertising agency has eight direct employees and a number of sub-contractors who are used to create much of the design work in line with very clear instructions and guidance by Emma and other members of staff.

This is a typical working day and Emma is out of the office for the next three days. When you sit down at your desk, you discover that a number of different items have been left in your in-tray by Emma for you to deal with.

1   Writing a brief speech from information supplied

Situation

From time to time Emma is asked to talk about advertising and marketing. She sees this as an excellent opportunity to reach the real decision makers in local businesses. For this reason, she places a great emphasis on getting the advertising message across. You will need to read her instructions in the memorandum and refer to her notes to help you put the five-minute speech together. Emma's hand-written notes can be found in Appendix A.

Emma Levy Advertising Associates

Memorandum

To: PA   From: EL

Re: Speech to Chamber of Commerce

On Friday next week I have been asked to speak at the monthly Chamber of Commerce meeting on the subject of Advertising. I want to be able to say how important advertising is and what its role is in business.

I have attached some hand-written notes for you, but I need you to put these together to create a five minute (no more than that I think) speech. The main point of the exercise is to tell them about advertising, I don't mind if you mention some of the things that it can't do, but be up-beat and positive for the most part.

Emma Levy

Assignment

Write up the speech for Emma and, if you feel that it is appropriate, include a simple chart or diagram outlining the main points that can either be used as a hand-out to the audience or as a transparency for an overhead projector.

(20 marks)

2   Writing a memorandum with a returnable slip for internal circulation

Situation

On a scrap of paper Emma has left you a note to remind you that the architects are coming into the office next week. At the last staff meeting she promised to circulate a form that would ask all the members of staff what they felt about open-plan offices. The intention is to knock down some of the partition walls and make a more attractive work space for all of the staff. This would mean that the senior members of staff would not have their own offices anymore, but would be given areas that could be partitioned off so that they could have meetings with clients in a secluded area of the office space.

Emma has asked you to write a memorandum to this effect for all of the staff and to design a simple form that could be filled in by them as a record of their comments about the plan.

You recall a recent conversation about the plan with Emma when she said: 'I have spoken to everyone about this, but they won't be pleased if I just make a decision without consulting them. At the end of the day, we need to improve the offices and I will only change my mind about it if there's some really valid reasons not to go open plan.'

Her note also cautions you not to say that the decision has really been made, but to make it clear that the open plan idea is a good one and that she is very keen to go ahead with it.

Assignment
Write a memorandum that addresses the above points and design a basic form that would allow the members of staff to make some comments about the proposal to go open plan.

(15 marks)

3 Preparing a notice and an agenda for a meeting

Situation
The meeting regarding the open plan office proposal is next week in the Board Room at 10.00 am, but Emma wants you to make it a part of a general staff meeting which can cover several points which she feels need discussion. As usual, the members of staff have sent in a number of requests that should be included on the agenda. The requests for items to be discussed can be found in Appendix B.

Emma has suggested that the following agenda items should be included: the open plan office proposal (including feedback from the staff), the new contract with Canwell Communications and the proposed staff weekend in Paris to celebrate the successful bid for the Mulligan Publishing account.

Assignment
Produce an agenda and notice of the meeting as requested.

(15 marks)

4 Producing an information sheet from information supplied

Following the circulation of the memorandum regarding the open-plan office proposal, you have received a number of comments back from the various members of staff. A summary of these can be found in Appendix C. You know that Emma will want you to summarise the comments and to try to show in your summary the strength of feeling and opinions, if possible.

Assignment

a   Using the comments in Appendix C, summarise the main points that have been made by the staff.

(15 marks)

b   Prepare a confidential memo for Emma noting which key members of staff are in favour of the open-plan proposal.

(15 marks)

Appendix A

Advertising Speech for the Chamber of Commerce

Advertising is often seen as a waste of money. It pushes up the prices that have to be passed on to the customer. It is, however, an enormous asset to businesses. Why?

Because:

You can use advertising to stimulate sales, this allows businesses to obtain extra income at times when sales are low or disappointing.

You can use advertising to stabilise sales at times when the business might be tempted to reduce prices to attract extra customers. After all, when sales pick up, you will only be tempted to increase the prices again.

You can use advertising to help to reduce the stocks that you are holding.

We all know how expensive it is to keep a high level of stocks, these costs will have to be passed on to the customer and it also ties up all of your capital. Advertising would help to lower the stock levels by generating a higher demand.

Hope this is of some use to you.

Appendix B

Emma Levy Advertising Associates

Memorandum

To: EL   From: LM

Re: Agenda Items for next staff meeting

I would like there to be some discussion about the lack of photocopying paper as this is causing extreme difficulties for the staff in the design department.

> # *Emma Levy Advertising Associates*
>
> **Memorandum**
>
> To: EL   From: KN
>
> <u>Re: Agenda Items for next staff meeting</u>
>
> Could you include a thank you for all of the staff that were involved in the recent meeting at Brondale Electronics. The work of the support staff and the designers was instrumental in the company beating off some strong competition from two other agencies.

Appendix C

'I think it's a great idea and I would find it far easier to supervise the staff.'
– Linda Mulligan, Design Manager

'I really think that it would mean a lot of extra noise and disruption to my work. If we did go open plan, I would want to have screens around me.'
– Kate Northover, Packaging & Promotions Manager

'The advantages in terms of work flow and communication would be great. I think that the open-plan system would really work for us in Client Fulfilment & Liaison.'
– Hassan Sanyari, Head of Client Fufilment & Liaison

'I really think that we will need some way of reducing the amount of noise that will be generated in one big space.'
– Felicity O'Mara, Receptionist

'I will be able to see everything that is going on, that's both good and bad!'
– Justine Davies, Production Controller

'The lack of privacy would be a real problem, especially when I'm trying to talk to clients. I don't think that it will be very professional if I keep having to ask people to keep the noise down.'
– Frank Forster, Client Fulfilment & Liaison

'There will be far more opportunities to be flexible about the way that we do things, I think it's a good idea.'
– Katie Harrison, Production Assistant

■ Written Practice Paper 2

General information applicable to all questions

(Information obtained from one question may be used in answering another.)

You work for Universal Paints & Solvents Ltd, which is housed on a small industrial estate just outside a market town in Essex. The job of receptionist is the most unpopular role in the organisation. As a way of getting around this problem, the Chief Administrative Officer, Clive Goodall, has requested that all employees of Administration Assistant grade take it in turns to be on reception. The rota is quite fair and you only have to cover the reception once every eight weeks for the whole of the week.

One of the reasons why the job is so unpopular is the fact that there is a constant stream of sales representatives visiting the company. Many of them do not have appointments but the company policy is that no one gets to see the buyers without an appointment. Some of the sales representatives are very difficult to get rid of and they get in the way of the normal work that has to be carried out by the receptionist.

It is the start of the week and it is your turn for the dreaded reception. You will need to handle a number of routine and non-routine activities during the course of the week.

1   Dealing with a difficult visitor

Situation

Unfortunately, one of the first visitors to the company this morning is a sales representative. He is very pushy and claims to be a close friend of the Managing Director, Kevin Johnson. The conversation (see Appendix A) does not go very well. Clearly, he is not impressed with you, the Managing Director's PA or the company. You will need to sort out the confusion and decide what you should do in this case.

Assignment

a   How would you deal with the problem and how would you make sure that the situation does not go any further (in terms of a potential complaint about your conduct)?

(10 marks)

b   To what extent do you think that the caller was responsible for the problem and how do you think that Georgina's comments helped to make the problem all the worse?

(10 marks)

2   Writing a letter with a returnable form for distribution to customers

Situation

After you have dealt with the first visitor, you now have a chance to look at the in-tray. There is a typed letter from a local hotel and some instructions regarding a launch event and party for customers. The company has just signed a deal to distribute some new American paints that can be mixed on the wall before they dry. This will be a very popular product line for DIY decorators who want to be able to give their walls special paint effects. The paints will be sold in the UK under the name of *Paintastik Effeks*.

The company has agreed the details included in the letter from the hotel regarding the catering and the function room, but you will need to draft a letter to the customers (this will be run through the database later and mail-merged). You will need to attach a return form that the customers can fill in to confirm their attendance and catering needs. The letter from the hotel can be found in Appendix B.

Assignment

Write a covering letter inviting the customers to the function. Also design a basic form that can be returned to your company accepting or declining the invitation and covering any other points that you feel are appropriate.

(20 marks)

3   Writing a confirmation letter and a memo

Situation

As part of the launch of the new paints, the Managing Director has decided that the reception area will be redecorated using *Paintastik Effeks* products. This will cause some disruption to the area, but should only take a day or so to complete. The redecoration has been timed to be done on the same day as the launch so that customers can come and see the paints in action. In order to ensure that the best effects are obtained from the products, the Managing Director has contacted a local interior design company to carry out the redecoration. You will need to write a confirmation letter to the company and produce a memorandum for circulation to all employees informing them about the redecoration.

The interior design company is called *Graham Cobb Interiors*. The address is 47 The High Street, Abridge, Essex, AB19 7GH. Your contact name for the company is Lawrence Britt.

Assignment

Produce a letter to be sent to *Graham Cobb Interiors* and a memorandum for circulation to all members of staff.

(15 marks)

4   Producing an information sheet from information supplied

The Product Development Manager has left a draft of an information leaflet, or press release, to be sent out to the media to coincide with the launch of the new range of paint products. His notes can be found in Appendix C. He assumes that you know the format for a press release and is relying on you to put together a draft for his approval. If he thinks that it is correct, then he will give it to the Managing Director for final approval.

Assignment

Create a draft press release based on the information contained in Appendix C.

(25 marks)

Appendix A

You: Good morning sir, welcome to Universal Paints & Solvents. How can I help you?

Visitor: I'm terribly late. Get Kevin Johnson on the phone and tell him that Harry Robins is here to see him.

You: I'm sorry Mr Robins, but before I do that I'll need to have your name and the company that you represent written down in the Visitor's Book. That's our company procedure.

Visitor: I haven't got time for all of that. I need to see Kevin now, so get him on the phone right now and tell him I'm here!

You: Just a moment. Will you please put your name and company into the Visitor's Book. I assume that you have an appointment?

Visitor: Oh, all right. I can see I'm getting nowhere here. You know that Kevin and I go back a long way? If you don't get him on the phone right now I'll see he gets to hear about it.

You: I'll call his PA while you're doing that.
  Georgina, hello. I've got a Mr Robins in reception and he is most insistent that he sees Mr Johnson right away. I have a note that he is out of the office until the afternoon, is that right? I thought so, but Mr Robins is saying that he is expected. There's no record of an appointment here either. What do you want me to do?

Georgina: *Just get rid of him. Kevin knew he was due this morning and tried to put him off. He's a real pain, but they're friends and he doesn't really want to hurt his feelings. You deal with it, OK?*

You: I'm sorry but Mr Johnson is unavailable. . .

Appendix B

Stamford Bridge Hotel
Harrison Lane, Abridge, Essex, AB1 4AN

Ms S. Bryant, Customer Services
Universal Paints & Solvents Ltd
Marchmont Industrial Estate
Abridge
Essex

24 April 199.

Dear Ms Bryant

Further to your enquiry of 19 April, can I confirm the following arrangements for your event to be held on 1 May at this hotel.

I can confirm that both the Wise Suite and the Minto Suite have been reserved for your exclusive use, and that we have set aside twenty rooms for your guests. The two suites offer you ample space for both the presentation and the static displays as you described.

Our head chef, Mr de Matteo, has confirmed that we are able to cater for the provisional figure of 50 guests, plus your own staff of 12, including any vegetarian requirements. Welcome drinks and appetisers will be available from 1.30pm as requested, with the buffet at 2.45pm, directly after your presentations. Our staff will be on hand for your guests and your own needs until 6pm.

I would be grateful for confirmation of the number of guests, particularly those who would wish to stay overnight at the hotel. I look forward to hearing from you.

Yours sincerely,

R. Gullit

Ruud Gullit, General Manager

Appendix C

Draft Press Release for *Paintastik Effeks* Launch

Exciting new paint products designed in the USA, but manufactured in the UK.

Launch date for UK sales is May 1st.

Major launch to trade customers at prestigious hotel in Essex.

Paints available in twenty colours.

Paints are not quick drying, they are designed to be mixed and matched on the wall for exciting new paint effects.

Paints manufactured by the leading UK paint specialist.

Available in 1, 2 and 5 litre cans.

Special range of paint effect brushes and pads compatible with the new paints.

The UK manufacturers will be using the new paints to re-design their reception on the launch day. Design by award-winning design company *Graham Cobb Interiors*.

■ Written Practice Paper 3

General information applicable to all questions

(Information obtained from one question may be used in answering another.)

You are employed as an Administrative Assistant by Westfolk County Council at one of their Community Centres. The services provided by the centre include the following:

- Youth Clubs (13–18 years) every Tuesday & Thursday night (start time 7.00 p.m., finish time 10.00 p.m.)
- Lunch Clubs (for the local High School which is next door to the centre) every Monday, Wednesday and Friday lunch time (12.00 p.m. to 2.00 p.m.)
- Women's Craft Group each Tuesday morning (10.15 a.m. to 12.00 p.m.)
- Young Unemployed Group each Friday afternoon (2.00 p.m. to 4.00 p.m.).

You work for the Senior Community Worker, Paula, who is in sole charge of the day-to-day activities of the Centre. There are two Youth Workers for each of the Youth Clubs, one additional 'counter assistant' for the Lunch Clubs and a cleaner.

Your main responsibilities are to assist Paula in carrying out all the administrative, publicity and book-keeping tasks associated with the centre. Your days are varied and you normally work from 9.30 a.m. to 5.30 p.m. each day.

1   Writing a letter

Situation

Paula has just received a letter of complaint from a local resident. Paula has received letters from this person before and he has proved to be very persistent in his complaints. Although he claims that he has contacted the police about the 'disturbances', experience has shown that the police pay little attention to him. Having said this, the complainant deserves a response from the centre. Paula has asked you to draft a letter replying to his complaint. She has asked you to be reassuring but not to say that he has reasonable grounds for his complaint. You know that the majority of the teenagers who use the centre are very quiet when they leave the centre at 10.00 p.m. The letter of complaint is in Appendix A.

Assignment

Write a suitable reply to the letter, taking into account the facts as you know them and the instructions that Paula has given you. Bear in mind that you should ensure that the reputation of the centre is up-held at all times.

(20 marks)

2   Producing minutes

Situation

A Centre Support Meeting was held yesterday afternoon to discuss the possibility of taking a group of Youth Club members to London for the weekend. You were present as the minutes secretary. Your normal practice is to tape the meeting and write up the minutes from the transcript. You have already typed up the transcript (this is printed in Appendix B).

Assignment

Using the transcript of the meeting in Appendix B, write up the minutes in an appropriate style.

(20 marks)

3   Writing a memorandum

Situation

Arising out of the meeting, Paula has prepared the information requested by Poppy. You will need to draft a memorandum, outlining the costs as Paula has suggested. Paula has also made an estimate of the miles that will be travelled, so you will need to work out the exact cost of the minibus hire charges so that the costs will be correct. This information is included in Appendix C.

Assignment

Produce a memorandum for the Support Group and work out the exact costings for the minibus hire.

(20 marks)

4   Producing a letter with a returnable slip

Situation
The Youth Club Members will need to be given a letter for their parents or guardians (where appropriate) to book their place on the trip to London. You should include in the letter the fact that the trip is educational and designed to give the members some practical skills in planning trips, budgeting and other activities. You should also say that the accommodation is basic and is self catering. You can decide on the start times and finish times for the trip over a weekend period. You should mention that the trip is being arranged and supervised by experienced Youth Workers and that those going on the trip will be covered by insurance. Paula will need to have the £10 in from those who wish to go as soon as possible. State in the letter that places are on a first come, first served basis. There are only 12 places available. The letter should only be given out to the girls, but you may wish to say that a similar trip will be organised for the boys.

Assignment
Write a letter for Paula to sign and include a separate form or slip for the Youth Club members' parents or guardians to fill in and sign.

(20 marks)

Appendix A

The Centre Manager
Leistworth Community Centre
Walpole Lane
Leistworth
Westfolk

12th June 199.

Dear Sir/Madam

I must again complain about the intolerable amount of noise generated by the youths using your centre. For the past three weeks, my wife and I have been woken up several times by motor cycles, shouting and screaming and other disturbances. This noise usually begins at about 9.30 at night and continues into the early hours of the morning.

I had thought that you were professional people and would not encourage the young tear-aways of the area to disturb local people in their own homes. On two occasions I have found considerable amounts of litter in my front garden after these disturbances.

I have spoken to the police about this matter on several occasions, but they have failed to arrest or caution any of the culprits. I feel that it is your responsibility to do something about the matter before the youths engage in any vandalism along Walpole Lane.

I demand immediate action now or I will put the matter in the hands of my solicitor and get the centre closed down for good. My wife's nerves are at breaking point and I am feeling the effects of many lost hours of sleep.

I look forward to your immediate reply and action on this matter.

Yours sincerely

Ronald Cruickshank

Appendix B

Centre Support Group Meeting 12th June 199–. 4.00 pm

Present: Poppy Katz (Chair); Peggy Smith (Support Group); Jack Whye (Support Group); Winston O'Gorham (Support Group); Paula Green (Centre Manager); Bill Beardshaw (Youth Worker); Angela Charles (Youth Worker)

Poppy Can I call the meeting to order please. Thank you everyone for coming, I know how difficult it is to get away from your other commitments for afternoon meetings. The only business this afternoon is to agree about the proposed trip to London. Paula has done a lot of the work on this so I'll ask her to explain what's been planned.

Paula Thank you Poppy. Well as you know, a lot of the local teenagers have never been to London. Angela and I have asked the Youth Club members whether they would like to spend a couple of days in the city so that they can experience travel, planning visits and catering for themselves.

Jack Can I butt in Paula? You say that you and Angela have asked the kids, does this mean that you are only proposing to take the girls on the trip? That's a bit sexist if you ask me.

Paula You're right that I want to take only girls. I don't think it's sexist, we would like to arrange something similar for the boys at a later date. If you had let me finish, I was about to explain that I did speak to Bill about this and he said that he would be tied up at weekends until the end of August. If we took boys, then I would really want to take a male Youth Worker along.

Jack Fair enough, sorry about jumping in, go on.

Paula I've worked out some preliminary costings on this and with some cash from the Centre funds we could offer the weekend to the members at around £10 each. They would have to put some money into a pot for the food. It would be self-catering at a Youth Hostel in the suburbs.

Peggy Would you be able to use the Community Bus? I understand that it works out fairly cheap compared to private mini-bus hire?

Poppy Yes, you're right. It's about 35p per mile I think. The insurance is fairly cheap too if we arrange it through the Council.

Angela Good idea, we'll look at that. The Community Bus seats 16, so that's 14 members plus Paula and me. I suppose that we can't really take 14 what with all of the bags and cases . . .

Jack   Knowing the girls, there'll be room for about three of them!

Paula   Let's be sensible about it, I reckon that if we take 12 there'll be plenty of room for all of the bags and other things.

Peggy   So how much do you need from the Centre's funds?

Angela   Well, we've worked out that there'll be about a £50 short-fall after we've taken everything into account.

Poppy   Any other questions – no? Then we'll put it to the vote. I think it's a great idea.

Jack   I'm for it if the boys get a chance to go some other time.

Bill   As soon as I get a free weekend I promise that I'll make myself available. I'm sorry I can't do it now, but I've only just moved house and weekends are my only chance to get the place straight.

Poppy   All in favour . . . that's unanimous. Thank you everybody and thank you to Paula and Angela for all their efforts and giving up a weekend, of course. Paula, could you let us have a full break down of all the costs so that we can see it in writing please? Thanks, I'll call the meeting closed at 4.30.

Appendix C

Costs
1   Accommodation will be paid by the Youth Club members (this is only £4.95 per night)
2   Accommodation for the two Youth Workers will be paid by the Out Reach Fund (this is £6.95 per night)
3   Youth Hostel Association Membership (£10) will be paid by the Council
4   Insurance costs 48p per person.
5   Minibus Hire Charges:

   For the first 100 miles – 45p per mile
   Thereafter – 35p per mile
   A full tank of fuel is provided, so there will be no extra cost.

Income
£10 per Youth Club Member as a contribution towards the accommodation and the insurance.

Apart from the minibus hire charges all other costs are covered.

Mileage Estimate

Leistworth to Youth Hostel	120 miles
2 round trips from Youth Hostel to tube station	30 miles
Sundry journeys	50 miles
Youth Hostel to Leistworth	120 miles

■ Written Practice Paper 4

General information applicable to all questions

(Information obtained from one question may be used in answering another.)

You are employed as an assistant to the Community Projects Manager of Lidburn Engineering Ltd. which is a major employer in the area.

The company has recently acquired four acres of land adjacent to the main factory. It is proposed to build a large storage facility on the new site as well as extending the car parking and lorry park area. It is also proposed that a staff canteen be built alongside the main factory on the existing car park. This development will free up considerable amounts of space in the present buildings so that the company can continue its ambitious expansion plans. There is also a possibility that the company could acquire another vacant site next to the newly purchased land upon which it is hoped that a second factory complex will be built in around five or ten years time.

Given the fact that the newly acquired land is on a 'green field site', there is some opposition to the expansion plans. To this end, the Community Projects Manager has been told to liaise with contacts in the local community to attempt to diffuse any potential opposition to the building proposal.

As the assistant to the Community Projects Manager, you know that you will be extremely busy and will need to ensure that everything that you do is correct. The company cannot afford to have the building plans delayed in any way.

1 Designing a questionnaire

Situation

The Community Projects Manager, Nikola Hart, has been asked to design a questionnaire that can be distributed to the local community in order to gauge their reactions to the proposed expansion programme.

Nikola has outlined the questions that she wants to ask (see Appendix A), but has left you to lay out the questionnaire so that the responses can be analysed quickly and effectively (this will probably be done by you anyway!).

Assignment

Referring to Appendix A, which contains the main questions Nikola wishes to ask the local community, design the questionnaire. It is proposed that the questionnaires are delivered to each home in the immediate area.

(20 marks)

2 Drafting a notice

Situation

As part of the on-going discussions and consultation with the local community, it is proposed that the company sets up an open meeting on 4 July at the Beeston Hall Hotel. The meeting will take place at 7.30 pm. The company will provide refreshments, an artist's impression of the new buildings and other information regarding the additional volume of traffic etc. The Managing Director, Joseph Adams, and several other members of the Board will be in attendance to answer questions arising from the meeting.

Assignment

Design a suitable notice for the purpose described.

(20 marks)

3 Writing a memorandum

Situation

Yesterday, three Lidburn Engineering Ltd. trucks used the high street in the local town as a short-cut to make sure that they got back to the factory before the end of their shift. Although there is no legal restriction regarding access along the high street, it is company policy that trucks do not use this route. Your boss, in the middle of trying to convince the local people that Lidburn's is a caring and considerate local business, has had to field at least ten complaints about the dangers and disruption caused by the trucks yesterday.

Your boss has asked you to draft a memorandum to the Distribution Manager advising him of yesterday's problems and to remind him of company policy.

Assignment

Write the memorandum to the Distribution Manager.

(20 marks)

4 Writing a letter

Situation

Following the problems with the three trucks yesterday, your boss has asked you to draft a letter to the ten or so complainants. In Appendix B there is a typical example of the complaints received (a letter hand-delivered to the factory last night).

Assignment

Write a suitable reply to the letter, taking into account the fact that the internal memorandum has been sent to the Distribution Manager. It is vital that the reputation of the company is maintained.

(20 marks)

Appendix A

Please organise the following questions in a logical order. It might be a good idea to have a mixture of different types of question format, including multiple choice:

How long have you lived in this area?

Do you have any connections with Lidburn Engineering Limited? If so, what is your connection with us?

Have you ever visited the site?

Have you ever visited the exhibition/building display at the local library?

Have you seen our posters advertising the consultation meetings with the public?

Do you have any objections regarding the development of the Lidburn site? If so, please state your objections.

Do you feel that the current site intrudes on your life in any way? Please give examples.

What are your feelings regarding the volume of traffic in the area?

Would you like to visit the site and be shown the new expansion and development proposals?

Do you feel that you have received sufficient information regarding the development of the site?

Appendix B

22 Orchard Close
Beeston

23rd June 199–

Dear Sirs

Yesterday afternoon, after picking up my children from school, I walked along the High Street. As you know, the High Street is narrow and not really suitable for cars, let alone larger vehicles. To my horror I saw no less than three of your articulated lorries slowly moving along the street weaving in and out of the parked cars and narrowly avoiding pedestrians.

I had no other alternative but to go into a shop with my children to avoid the first truck as it mounted the kerb near to where we were walking. My children were terrified and I know that we were not the only ones.

I had thought that your company did not encourage your drivers to use the High Street as a short-cut, but I was obviously wrong. I am disgusted with your lack of concern for the town and the local people.

I look forward to hearing your comments and explanations.

Yours faithfully,

Brenda Jefferies

■ Written Practice Paper 5

General information applicable to all questions

(Information obtained from one question may be used in answering another.)

You work as an administration officer in a College. You are primarily concerned with student services, particularly organising the travel arrangements to and from the College for the students in the more remote areas of the county.

In the past, the service was paid for and provided by the County Council. However, due to the cuts in service, the Council now pays 75 per cent of the costs and has suggested that this will be reduced to 50 per cent next year. The College has, however, pledged that they will cover the funding short-fall for the foreseeable future.

Perhaps the most important consideration is the administration side of the funding changes. Whilst the County Council is still prepared to contribute 75 per cent of the costs, they have made the College Transport section of the Education Department redundant. This means that the College will have to be responsible for the administration function.

1   Writing a letter with a tear-off return slip

Situation
Although the change in funding will not affect the students, the College needs to inform them about the switching over of the administration function. This letter should have the dual function of requiring the students or their parents/guardians to inform you of the pick-up point.

Assignment
Write the standard letter with the tear-off slip as required.

(20 marks)

2   Organising a cover schedule

Situation
Amongst your other tasks, you are required to organise cover for the enquiry desk. This is always a difficult task since the demands on the other members of the administration team are as onerous as your own. Each of the ten administration officers are required to cover the enquiry desk for at least two days a month. Given a normal month, with 20 working days, this is the fairest way of organising and allocating the work.

Assignment
Create a list detailing who will cover the enquiry desk for each day of the month – you will need to refer to the memoranda contained in Appendix A. Note that all of the memoranda refer to the working days of the month that they are committed to other duties and will not be able to cover the enquiry desk. It is common practice that no one covers the enquiry desk for two consecutive days. Note that the total number of working days for the month is 20.

(20 marks)

3   Writing a memorandum

Situation
Having produced a letter to be sent to all students, you need to ensure that the teaching staff remind the students that they should return these forms as soon as possible.

Assignment
Write a memorandum to all staff outlining the changes in funding and the implications and stress that they need to ensure that all of the students return their tear-off slips.

(20 marks)

4 Producing a timetable

Situation

There has had to be some re-organisation of the coach routes in order to cut costs. To this end, you have requested information from the coach hire company regarding the travel times on one of the main routes which needs reviewing. They have supplied you with the travel times between the different pick-up points (see Appendix B). You will have to work out the exact pick-up times based on the assumption that the coach should arrive at the College no later than 8.40 a.m. On the return journey, the coach will leave the College at 4.40 p.m.

Assignment

Create a timetable for both the pick-ups (incoming coach journey) and the drop-offs (outgoing coach journey).

(20 marks)

Appendix A

From:	Mandy
	I cannot cover the enquiry desk on days 9–14. I will be on a training course.

From:	Rachel
	I cannot cover the enquiry desk on days 1, 4, 7 and 10. I have to cover student enrolments on those days.

From:	Terry
	I cannot cover the enquiry desk from day 15 as I will be on holiday.

From:	Mary
	I have no commitments this month.

From:	Jo
	I cannot cover the enquiry desk on days 5–9 and 18–20. I am taking these days as part of my annual leave.

From:	Louise
	I cannot cover the enquiry desk for the first half of the month (until day 11, I will be working at the annex).

From:	Harry
	I cannot cover the enquiry desk on days 12–15 this month, I have to do the school visits.

From:	Penny
	I cannot cover the enquiry desk for the first five days of the month.

From:	Sherri
	I have no other commitments this month and can cover the enquiry desk on any day of the month.

You yourself have commitments on the Thursday and Friday of each week, in other words, you cannot cover the enquiry desk on days 4, 5, 9, 10, 14, 15, 19 & 20.

Appendix B

Yardley Lane	Start point
Neath Street	5 minutes
Heath Road	10 minutes
Getsford	10 minutes
Trinfleet	5 minutes
Ofland	5 minutes
Uggesford	10 minutes
Swanhead	5 minutes
Ilkeshall	5 minutes
Spexham	5 minutes
College	Finish point

■ Oral Assignment Practice Paper 1

Assignment for a business telephone call

Situation

You work as an administrative assistant in the busy sales department of a toy manufacturer and importer called Blackburn Toys & Games Ltd. The company occupies three industrial units on the York Hall Trading Estate, Tottenham Hale, London. Your immediate boss is the sales manager Bernard Gross. He spends about half of his time on the road with the sales representatives and the other half engaged in administrative duties. The company has been operating for over twelve years and has a good reputation with the customers.

Tutor role

In the role of Margaret Britton, a representative from the Real Toys Ltd chain of toy and game shops, you are expecting a call from Blackburn Toys & Games Ltd explaining why your appointment with Bernard Gross was cancelled only two hours before you were due to discuss a major order you wished to place with the company, following your visit to their trade stand at a Toy & Game Fair. Luckily, you have a car phone and your office managed to get a message to you after you were half way to Blackburn Toys & Games Ltd premises in Tottenham. You are angry and need to be convinced that you should not place the order elsewhere.

Task

You should refer to Appendix 1 which contains the note left by Bernard Gross on the matter. He is not in the office and he has left you to deal with the situation.

Assignment for a business interview

Situation

You work as an administrative assistant in the busy sales department of a toy manufacturer and importer called Blackburn Toys & Games Ltd. In the absence of your boss, Bernard Gross, you are expected to take responsibility for the sales representatives. You are required to deal with a new sales representative who has only been with the company for three months. Each of the sales representatives are expected to visit at least six customers per day. During the first two days of this week, the sales representative, Terry Worthington, was not contactable. You had several messages for him, but were unable to get these messages to him until the day before yesterday. Bernard has asked you speak to Terry and resolve the situation. A short profile of Terry is included in Appendix 2.

Tutor role

In the role of Terry Worthington, you should try to explain that your car phone was not working and that you did not have the chance to call into the office to see if there were any messages for you. You should also explain that you do not know your sales territory very well and that you have got lost on several occasions. You should accept the advice that is given to you as you are aware of the fact that you are on six months trial with the company.

Task

After requesting that Terry comes into the office to see you, you have been left by Bernard to resolve the situation. Specifically, Bernard wants the following points made:

- that Terry should check in with the office at least twice a day
- that Terry should send in, fax or telephone the office to tell them where he is and which customers he has visited each day
- that Terry should try to learn the best routes around his sales territory and be rather more systematic about his visits (he seems to be driving without a clear plan of covering the same area on a particular day)
- that Terry still has three months of his trial period to work
- that Terry has to account for his whereabouts at all times during working hours.

Assignment for a business presentation

Situation

Bernard Gross, your boss, has asked you to begin the preparations for the annual sales conference. This important function, which gives all of the sales representatives the opportunity to meet with one another, is held in June. The normal practice is to choose a hotel in one of the regions so that it is not necessary to make all of the representatives come down to London each time.

The guests of honour will be the local MP, Jennifer Macdonald, and the company's first director (now retired), Harold Blackburn. To commemorate the continued success of the Hedgehog Family range of toys and games, Harold will be presented with a special edition of the game (now in its tenth year of sales).

To assist you in the preparation of the conference, which only lasts for a day, there are two other clerical assistants who have been temporarily moved into the sales department for this sole purpose.

Task

You are required to prepare a short presentation to your boss of what is proposed. The presentation should cover some of the following aspects of the conference:

- how you propose to timetable the event
- the delegation of responsibility in the following areas:
    - the greeting of the guests
    - organising the food and drink
    - dealing with emergency calls from customers during the day
    - arrangements necessary for the smooth-running of the conference
    - transport between the venue and the train station
    - the details of the presentation to Harold Blackburn.

Further details are included in Appendix 3.

You will be expected to clarify any points which may arise.

Appendix 1

Can you please explain to Margaret Britton that I was unavoidably detained in Sheffield on the 23rd. Tell her that I must admit that my meeting with her slipped my mind in the rush to sort out a problem up north.

Tell her that I will willingly visit her at her own office to suit her. Try to reassure her that we are committed to providing a high quality of customer service and that this is just one occasion when the system broke down.

We will, of course, reimburse her for any expenses that she incurred as a result of the wasted journey. Can you arrange a meeting at her office as soon as possible and I will rearrange my diary to suit her.

Remember that she is a key customer and we do not want to lose her business.

Thanks

Bernard

Appendix 2

Blackburn Toys & Games Ltd
Appraisal Form

Name: Terence Worthington
Age: 23
Job Title: Sales Representative

A positive and reliable young man with a good commitment to the company. This is his second job since leaving college with an HND in Business. He is generally liked by the other sales representatives, but his age does cause some problems with the older reps.

He has managed to increase the sales revenue in the area by 3 per cent in the first two months of his employment.

He confesses that he is having trouble finding his way around the territory, but is gradually managing to organise himself.

It is the sales manager's opinion that he needs close supervision for the first few months, but should be a valuable addition to the sales force.

Appendix 3

Events, speeches and presentations:

- Sales speech by the sales manager (thirty five minutes)
- Opening address by the managing director (ten minutes)
- Explanation of the new accounting procedures by the accounts director (twenty minutes)
- Speech by Jennifer Macdonald MP (approx. fifteen minutes)
- Presentation of the special edition game to Harold Blackburn (five minutes)
- Question & answer session for the sales representatives (fifteen minutes)
- Speeches by the three area sales managers (fifteen minutes each)
- Coffee break (around 10.30 am twenty minutes)
- Lunch break (around 1.30 pm one hour)
- Tea break (around 4.00 pm twenty minutes)
- Time set aside for the reps to see the new product ranges (forty minutes)

■ Oral Assignment Practice Paper 2

Assignment for a business telephone call

Situation

You work in a training agency in Norwich as an administration supervisor. Broadland Business Training Ltd actually consists of four management and supervisory trainers with a support staff of three. Your immediate boss is the training co-ordinator, and you have an administrative assistant to aid you in your work. The four trainers are the owners of the company with three owning 20 per cent of the shares each and the remaining trainer, Bernice Dempsey, owning the remaining 40 per cent. The offices are small, but they are situated in the centre of the city.

Tutor role

In the role of Bernice Dempsey, who is usually a well-organised and efficient individual, contact the candidate by telephone and explain that you have left some important papers concerning a client on your desk. Note the names, times and job titles with the candidate (inserting an error which should be corrected by the candidate). The candidate should also make reference to the telephone message taken by the training co-ordinator.

Task

You should refer to Appendix 1 which contains the information from Bernice Dempsey's desk as well as the telephone message.

Assignment for a business interview

Situation

You work as an administration supervisor for Broadland Business Training Ltd, which operates in Norfolk. You have been asked by your boss, the training co-ordinator, to carry out the preliminary interviews for a new vacancy with the company. Due to the expansion of the business, it has been decided to give you extra help and this has created another post for an administrative assistant. The details of one of the candidates is included in Appendix 2.

Tutor role

In the role of Laura Jones, you will be interviewed by the candidate. You should try to explain why you have applied for the job and how you think that your skills and abilities would be an asset to the company. You are rather shy and the candidate should have to work quite hard to get information from you.

Task

The candidate should interview the job seeker and attempt to get the following answers:

■ Why have you applied for this job?
■ What do you know about the company?

- What skills and knowledge do you have that could be useful?
- What training would the job seeker need?

Assignment for a business preparation

Situation

The training partners have decided that they need to up-date their initial presentation material to potential clients. They also feel that you have the potential to become a trainer in the future. As a result, they have prepared the basic information that they want to be translated into a series of flip charts, OHTs or some other visual image. They would like you to create these and talk them through your explanation of the information as if you were presenting these to a new client. This is an excellent opportunity for you to show them what you can do.

Task

Using the details that are included in Appendix 3, create a series of visual images that could be used by the company when making the initial presentation to a new client. Your tutor will take the role of the partners and will ask you questions about the ways in which you have presented the information.

Appendix 1

Absol Ltd

Arrive @ Ipswich 2.30. There is no parking near the company, so allow extra time to walk from the multi-storey car park in the centre of the town.

Meet Henry Makepeace in reception @ 3.15. Full meeting with MD (Bryan Macdonald), Finance Director (Marlene Graham) and the Administration Director (Judy MacNab) @ 3.30.

They are mainly interested in team-building as well as some IT training.

Key personnel (notes taken from the last visit to the company):

- Bryan – quite friendly, pre-occupied with other things, will probably go along with the rest of the directors.
- Marlene – has a number of problems with her staff and is very keen on training.
- Judy – has had to make several staff redundant following the introduction of new IT applications, keen to rebuild her teams.
- Henry – quite hostile to outsiders, would really like to organise the training himself.

Should finish @ 5.00

Telephone message

From: Henry Makepeace
To: Bernice Dempsey

We are not convinced that we need team building training. Have spoken to Bryan about this and we will probably decide to do it in-house.

Appendix 2

Laura Jones	

Age: 19

Qualifications: RSA Secretarial Certificate
NVQ level 3 Admin.
5 GCSEs above C

Previous Employment:

2 weeks work experience with local engineering company in their finance department

2 weeks work experience with Marks & Spencer mainly in personnel and administration

6 months (temporary contract covering maternity leave) with County Council in the administration section of personnel

Currently unemployed.

Other details: Has recent knowledge of education and training. Interested in this area of work. Quite flexible. Car owner/driver. No family commitments.

Appendix 3

Key notes for initial client presentations

Small, local training consultancy.
Over twenty years combined experience.
Key trainers are the owners of the company.
Personalised training a speciality.
Individual training, group or company-wide training offered.
Seeking to establish a long-term relationship with the client.
Always available for short-notice training needs.
Prepared to install short-term in-house trainers when required
Operates throughout the East Anglia region.
Able to offer training on the latest technological developments.
Experienced trainers from a variety of business backgrounds.
A long list of satisfied customers and able to show testimonials.

■ Oral Assignment Practice Paper 3

Assignment for a business telephone call

Situation

You work in the accounts department of a family-owned supermarket. Your specific duties include organising the payroll for the whole of the organisation. It is computerised and the vast majority of the employees are paid one month in arrears directly into their bank accounts. The casual workers, who normally work weekends and the occasional evening, are paid weekly in cash.

All of the casual workers must pick up and sign for their wage packets between 5.00 and 7.00 p.m. on a Friday night and they are paid one week in arrears. The procedure strictly states that the employee must only sign if they are satisfied that they have received the correct pay. It is company policy not to accept any complaints arising out of a particular pay packet once it has been signed for.

Tutor role

In the role of a parent of one of the Saturday workers, you should contact the candidate by telephone and inform them that their son/daughter's pay packet was £5.00 short this week. They should have received £15.00, but there was only £10.00 in the wage packet. The pay advice slip states that the payment was £15.00.

Task

You should politely but firmly state the company policy on wage payments and the signing off procedure to the parent.

Assignment for a business interview

Situation

The problem with the wage packet was unresolved following the telephone conversation. The parent insists on coming into the shop and talking to either you or the manager about the situation. Since the responsibility is yours, the shop manager insists that you handle the situation, but tells you that you must repeat company policy and that under no circumstance should you give the parent the disputed £5.00.

Before the meeting with the parent, you get the opportunity to talk to the son/daughter to see if you can shed more light on the situation. The content of that discussion is in Appendix 1.

Tutor role

In the role of the parent, you must insist that the candidate makes up the missing amount from your son/daughter's wage packet. If pressed, you will state that you would prefer your son/daughter to leave the company's employ rather than let the company get away with under-paying. You will also threaten to inform the police and your MP.

Task
You have the difficult task of dealing with the parent as well as informing them of the content of the conversation with their son/daughter. You should be as tactful as possible.

Assignment for a business presentation

Situation
Arising out of the problem with the wage packet, the shop manager has asked you to list a series of proposals aimed at making sure that a similar situation does not arise again. He realises that it is impossible to pay the casual staff in any other way than in cash, but he would like you to research some security measures that could be adopted in the future.

Task
You should make a short presentation to the manager of the shop outlining the new procedures that you would like to use in order to ensure that a similar situation does not arise again in the future.

computerised system. You really need to know what information they need to have and the best way to get it to them when they need it. You should bear in mind that the sales representatives operate from home and are on the road for most of the week. The primary means of communication during working hours is by mobile phone.

Tutor role

In the role of one of the sales representatives, you will be interviewed by the candidate who will ask you about your needs for a computerised stock control and ordering system. You should stress that you need accurate and up-to-date information regarding the stock situation of the brands of shoes as well as the manufacturing completion dates so that you can tell the stockists when they can expect the deliveries. You would prefer to have direct access to the system and have some way of being able to 'pre-order' the stock so that the correct number of pairs of shoes are always available.

Task

Interview the sales representative and make notes regarding their needs in respect of the proposed computerised system.

Assignment for a business presentation

Situation

Having carried out your research regarding the computerised system, you will now need to present your findings to the Managing Director. The Managing Director is fully aware of the fact that the systems need to be overhauled and updated, but needs to have a compelling reason to make the necessary investment. You should expect to be questioned regarding the ease of use and the access to the system. It is the Managing Director's final decision whether the system is purchased and you know that the company really needs to make the investment.

Task

You should make a short presentation to the Managing Director, outlining the proposed purchase of the computerised system. You will need to mention the benefits of the system to the company and the rough costs. The Managing Director will be keen to ensure that the sales representatives are fully trained to use the system and that some level of training is included in your proposal.

Appendix 1

Telephone Message

From: Midlands Sales Representatives
To: Administrative Assistant, Production & Stores Department

Preliminary discussions with customers show that we will need to deliver the following (approx.) numbers of the following as soon as possible:

Clarissa   50
Madeline   60
Alessa   25
Andrea   40
Josie   35

I will call you to confirm the number of days before delivery can be made.

Stock/Production summary

	Current Stock	Ready in 5 Days	Ready in 10 Days
Alessa	20	15	15
Andrea	30	10	10
Beatrice	10	—	20
Clarissa	25	15	15
Dessie	30	30	30
Flora	20	20	20
Josie	40	10	10
Lillian	10	10	10
Madeline	20	10	10
Majestic	30	—	—
Nana	20	10	10
Sophia	15	10	10
Veronica	30	—	10
Williamina	20	10	20
Zoe	30	20	20

The delivery time from the factory to the customer is 48 hours by road carrier.

■ Oral Assignment Practice Paper 5

Assignment for a business telephone call

Situation

You work for an employment agency, Matthew Whitmore Employment. Your main duties are administrative, but you are also required to carry out a number of other duties, including registering individuals who wish to be potential employees for the agency's business clients. It is a busy office in the centre of a city and the work is varied and interesting most of the time.

The agency has just submitted five potential candidates for a secretarial post with one of your major clients. Unfortunately, you have been given the responsibility to tell the unsuccessful candidates that they have not been offered the job. This is the first time that you have had to do this, but you do have some details from the client so that you can give some feedback to the unsuccessful candidates in the hope that it may be of some use to them in the future.

Tutor role

In the role of one of the unsuccessful candidates, you will be at first surprised and then rather upset that you have not been offered the job. You should question the decision that has been made and take issue with some of the comments that the candidate is feeding back from the client. You should be forceful and assertive at all times.

Task

Using Appendix 1, which contains the feedback information from the client, make the call to the unsuccessful candidate and inform them that they have not been offered the job. Note that there may be statements in the feedback document that the candidate should not be appraised of for legal reasons.

Assignment for a business interview

Situation

Although the majority of individuals who register with the agency have secretarial experience, there are a number who have skills in other areas. Some have had considerable experience in a number of different posts over the years, but do not have any formal qualifications. The standard procedure is to attempt to fill in the pro-forma registration form during an informal interview with the individual after they have decided whether to register with the agency. Once the form has been completed, one of the employment advisers will re-interview the individual and try to match their skills against one or more of the current vacancies. It is essential that the form is filled in as correctly and completely as possible.

Tutor role

In the role of an individual who wishes to register with the agency (see notes in Appendix 2), you will be interviewed by the candidate. You should let the candidate ask all of the questions and only respond to them. You should not volunteer any information about yourself unless you have been asked specifically for that information.

Task

Interview the individual and attempt to complete the pro-forma registration form (Appendix 3) to the best of your ability.

Assignment for a business presentation

Situation

You have been asked by the company to carry out the preliminary planning for attendance at an employment fair at the local college. This could be a useful connection for the agency and there is also the opportunity to make contact with some of the other local employers in the area. The agency is keen to have a high profile at the college event and one of the owners of the agency has suggested that the agency offers to sponsor the event or carry out some other marketing proposal that will help the students and local employers remember the name of the agency.

Task

You should make a short presentation to the Managing Director which details the planning that the agency will have to do in order to make their attendance at the event a successful one. You should be prepared to offer some ideas about marketing or the possible advantages and disadvantages of sponsoring the event.

Appendix 1

Feedback Sheet

Although this individual was a strong candidate for the post, we had some reservations regarding the commitment and willingness to carry out other duties other than the secretarial responsibilities.

We also felt that the age of the candidate (over thirty) meant that they would not fit in with the younger age group of employees that we would wish to take on.

The candidate did not appear to be as well prepared as we would have liked and lacked some communication skills that we would have expected. In this respect at least two of the other candidates were stronger verbally and seemed to be able to cope with the questioning better.

In terms of the candidate's skills and qualifications, on paper, we were satisfied. But in-depth questioning led us to understand that the candidate had not worked as a secretary in the recent past and we were concerned that her skills and abilities would be rather rusty.

We also felt that the candidate could have made a greater effort to be more presentable for the interview and was concerned that the candidate would not look as well-groomed and dressed as we would have liked.

The candidate did not appear to be very well appraised of the nature of the work carried out by our company and did not really appear to be very interested in finding out from us what we actually do.

Having said this, the candidate was considerably better than two of the others but was not in the same league as the candidate we offered the post to, or second choice for the post.

Appendix 2

Candidate details (for Tutor use)

You are 24.

You live at 10 Station Road.

You have three children.

You have a driving licence.

You live within ten miles of the agency.

You are prepared to travel into the city for a job.

You have been unemployed for three months.

You have worked since leaving school at sixteen.

You worked for a major bank for three years and was then made redundant. Your job role was that of cashier and customer service adviser. You can type, but you are self taught.

You have 6 GCSEs at Grade C or better.

You have no other formal qualifications.

For the past three years, you have temped for other agencies in the area, including work in administration (1 year), reception (3 months), accounts (6 months), stock control (3 months) and factory work (various for 1 year).

You were referred to this agency by a friend who obtained a full-time job through them.

You do not wish to work in accounts or stock control again, but would consider any other post.

Appendix 3

Registration Card
Name:
Address:
Age:
Dependants:
Driving licence: Yes/No
Qualifications:
Other skills:
Previous experience:
Job likes/ dislikes:
Heard of by?
Other details:

Index